# A JOURNEY IN TIME

## *Mendocino County*
## WILDFLOWERS

Peter W. Stearns

PWS

**A Journey In Time**: *Mendocino County Wildflowers*
Copyright © 2003 and 2007 by Peter W. Stearns

**Peter W. Stearns Enterprises**
215 West Standley Street
Ukiah, California 95482
707-463-6643
pstearns@pacific.net
www.peterwstearns.com


Book Design: Michael Brechner / Cypress House
Cover Design: Gopa and Ted 2

**Publisher's Cataloging-in-Publication Data**

Stearns, Peter W., 1928-
  A journey in time : Mendocino county wildflowers / Peter W. Stearns.
-- 2nd ed. -- Ukiah, CA : Peter W. Stearns Enterprises, 2006.
    p. ; cm.
  ISBN-13: 978-0-9773049-2-9
  ISBN-10: 0-9773049-2-2
  First ed. published: Fort Bragg, CA : Cypress House, © 2003.
  Includes index.
    1. Wild flowers--California--Mendocino County--Pictorial works.
2. Nature photography--California--Mendocino County. 3. Stearns,
Peter W., 1928- I. Title.
  QK149 .S74 2006
  582.13/09794/15 0601                    2005909261

Printed in China

2    4    6    8    9    7    5    3    1

# A JOURNEY IN TIME

*Mendocino County Wildflowers*

*Peter W. Stearns in his natural habitat*

*I* dedicate A Journey In Time *to all those people who came before me, who are with me now, and who will follow me, for their passion and vision in saving the "wildness" of our planet's wildflowers, in this case, the flowers of Mendocino County.*

*I dedicate this book to the courage of the nameless individuals who stand as sentinels, vigilant in preserving the precious natural world and the many life forms we share it with.*

*I dedicate this book to all those who gather strength from the beauty and enjoyment they receive from nature's benign gift of wildflowers, freely given.*

Some long-forgotten place
Of mind and soul
Is pierced with shafts of light
And for an instant
Lifts a veil on hidden wonders
Of things
Once known and understood.

*— Peter W. Stearns*

# CONTENTS

# INTRODUCTION

MENDOCINO COUNTY is an incredibly diverse region. The height of the mountains in the northeast section of the inner coastal range varies from 6,000 feet to the highest point in the county, the 7,200-foot summit of Anthony Peak. The inner valleys, such as Round Valley, Willits, Potter Valley, and Ukiah, range in elevation from 700 to 1,700 feet. The outer mountains of the coastal range, near the coast, reach 2,900 feet. Mendocino County's coastline runs unbroken for more than 120 miles.

The environment within the county's borders supports a variety of plant and animal communities. The features of Mendocino's diversity will come into focus as I describe the various areas and habitats where "our" wildflowers are found. Since geology — the makeup of the Earth's crust in a given region — determines the environment where plants and animals flourish, I've included several paragraphs on geology. I describe three belts of rocks: the eastern belt, where our higher-elevation flowers are found; the middle belt, where grassland and rolling-hill flowers grow; and the western belt, where coastal and redwood flowers flourish.

This book contains 313 images of plants; the common names of plants are followed by their Latin names (genus and species) throughout, giving botanists and wildflower purists worldwide the same name for each plant wherever it may be found. Most of them are considered native plants (indigenous plants that occur naturally in an area, rather than as direct or indirect consequences of human activity). I include plants that have escaped from cultivation, from gardens, and from other parts of the world. I identify these as such and name the region they came from. I've excluded many of the obnoxious alien plants that threaten our native plants and their habitat. I include a few of these, however, since they are well established and attract our attention to their color and location (see photograph #16, page 17).

This is a book about Mendocino County wildflowers and the wondrous, magical place they inhabit. As a young boy, I spent a number of summers in the Adirondack Mountains in the upper Saranack Lake region of New York State. I learned to see things through the eyes of a seventy-five-year-old Adirondack guide named George Colin. Those years between 1934 and the beginning of the Second World War set my imagination and eyes forever on the clarity and richness of nature. I have carried George's lessons with me all my life, and would like to pass them on to you.

I see in the beauty of wildflowers a capsule of time, a way to look back into the past and to look toward the future. It is imperative that we humans share our planet equally with all other life forms. We need to view our world like children, with wonder and delight. Wildflowers and other life forms and the places they inhabit are vanishing at an alarming rate. We must learn to slow down and become still, to be quiet observers of life, careful with the things around us — the plants, the animals, and the air we breathe.

The photography in this book is mine. I am only a conduit of things that nature allows me to receive. I capture nothing; the camera and film are merely devices that see and record what has always been there — a marvelous world of light and beauty. On these pages I have mixed landscapes and flowers into a tapestry of Nature's own design. I have tried to blend the task of identifying and labeling wildflowers with portraying their innate beauty. As a photographer, I hope I've been able to convey to you the sense of receiving images rather than of capturing them.

Many parts of Mendocino County are still unspoiled, and there is a feel of timelessness, of quiet places to walk, to sit, and observe. In this book, most of the images of wildflowers and landscapes may be seen from your car or by walking a short distance into the woods and fields. For your pleasure I have included my heartfelt observations on each month as we journey through the year.

It is my intention to have you follow a season of wildflowers that begins each year in January and lasts until December. My wife Robbie and I have watched and followed this rebirth of life with awed enchantment. This book is about the magic and beauty that exist in and around us each and every day. Let us start our journey together.

*Peter W. Stearns*

# HOW TO USE THIS BOOK

A *JOURNEY IN TIME* is a book of photographs and text presenting a cycle of wildflowers that bloom from January through December each year. The photographs of the wildflowers have been arranged by month in the order in which they first bloom. In most cases, I've listed the earliest blooming time for each species of flower, with the understanding that the cycle of bloom may continue for a month or more. Thus, if you're using the book in the county during the month of June, it's wise to look at the months of April and May as well as the following month of July.

Whenever possible, the flowers that are found growing in a specific type of habitat have been placed on the same flower pages. Each month's flowers are arranged by habitat from east to west, progressing from the inner mountains to the foothill woodlands, inner valleys, redwoods, and finally the coast.

All the flowers were photographed in the habitat where they grow, using only natural light. I chose to concentrate on the flowers' shape and color, leaving out much of the background. I suggest observing the flowers from a distance of six to twenty-four inches. Carry a magnifying glass for closer work. This distance is consistent with the scale of the photographs in the book.

The letters "**A / S**" following the Latin name stand for *actual size*. When **A / S** appears, it means the photograph you are looking at is approximately the same size as the flower you are looking for. The image of the Fetid Adder's Tongue in photograph #1 for January is shown as **2 × A / S**, meaning the photograph is twice the actual size of the flower. The Rhododendron shown in photograph #157 (page 95) for May is **¹/₃ A / S**. The size of all flowers differs within the same species, so I've added a plus (**+**) or a minus (**–**) after the **A / S** to allow for some variation between the image and the flower.

On the description page opposite the flower photographs, I've given the common name or names along with the Latin name, and have provided a **When**, **Where**, and **What** for each flower. **When** is the approximate time during a given month that you'll see the flower in bloom. **Where** includes the range and type of habitat in which you may expect to find the flower blooming. I've included specific places to look for flowers to give you examples of like places found in other areas of the county. **What** will give you a brief description of the plant and the family it belongs to. I included the Latin name after each common name so that you can search for more technical information in professional botanical books if you so choose.

The bonus you receive from this book will come from nature itself and the incredible diversity and beauty it provides for its wildflowers. We have spent much time looking inward; I hope that in the process we have learned to look outward with a deeper appreciation of the world we live in and the many life forms that share our world with us.

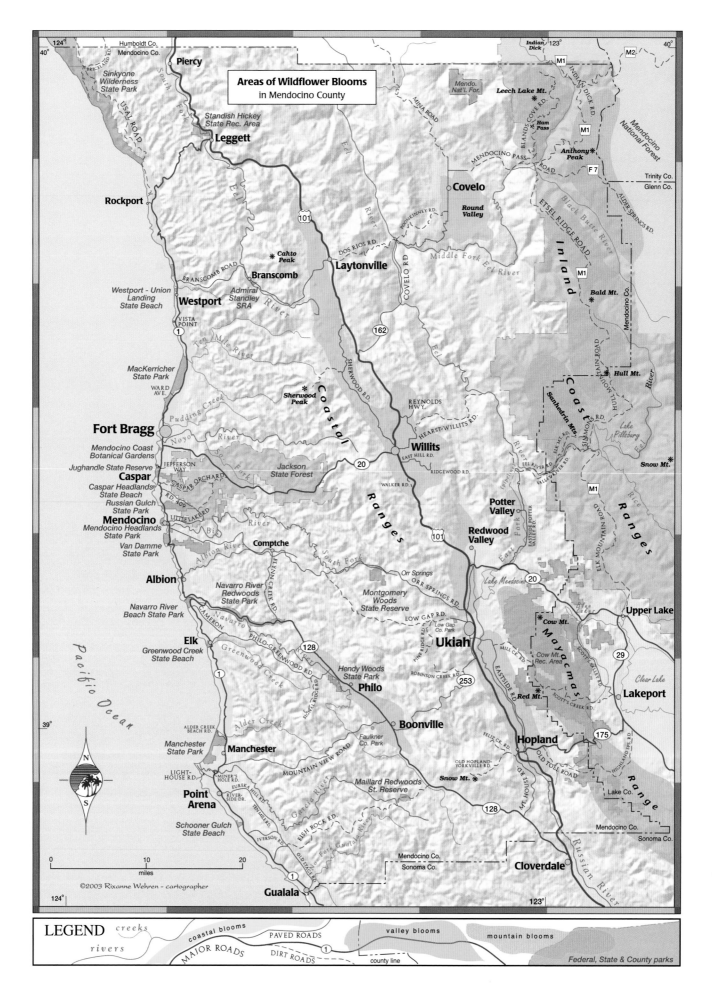

Areas of Wildflower Blooms
in Mendocino County

4

# GEOLOGY OF MENDOCINO COUNTY

MENDOCINO COUNTY is within the California Coast Range. The Coast Range is relatively young by geological time. There are three belts of a complex suite of rocks called the Franciscan Assemblage. These belts stretch the length of the county, running from the southeast to the northwest, and are placed side by side across the width of the county, from the coast to our eastern boundary.

(1) The coastal belt rocks are sedimentary rocks that support our redwood forests and coastal plains.

(2) The central belt rocks, exposed in the Ukiah Valley in Low Gap County Park, are also sedimentary but contain red and green chert (very tough, fine-grained rock), serpentine, and green schists (metamorphic rocks containing parallel layers of flaky minerals). Serpentines, (rock composed primarily of a hydrated magnesium silicate), in California are noted for harboring a diverse array of endemic plant species.

(3) The eastern belt rocks intermix with the central belt rocks in the vicinity of Sanhedrin Mountain. The eastern belt to our north encompasses the highest mountains in the county. The rocks in the eastern belt are more metamorphosed (heated and changed). They include sandstone and shale that grade into slates and schists, giving them a shiny silvery color. Many other exotic metamorphic and volcanic rocks are present in the eastern belt and to an extent the central belt. Within the central and eastern belts are house-sized boulders, called *tectonic knockers,* which float (resembling icebergs) in a matrix of clay. This unlikely mixture is called a melange (matrix is a mix of rock ground down to sand and clay). Within this area of lower, grass-covered rolling hills and woodlands, many of our colorful spring and early summer wildflowers are found.

# JANUARY

S oft winter light brushes the landscape into shades of brown and gray. The peaceful solitude of the forests and grassland hills contrasts with the windswept coast and restless sea. In the high country, the inner mountains are deep in slumber, frosted with snow. Winter has arrived in Mendocino County. Storms from the Pacific Ocean and the Gulf of Alaska sweep into northern California with unabated fury, and yet January is when our journey begins.

It seems unlikely that a flower would choose this month to make an appearance, but we learn with delight that the annual rebirth and blooming cycle commences now and continues through the year into December. The anticipation of a new wildflower season is a marvelous way to start the year. The sense of new beginning and celebration of life is as timeless as the universe we inhabit. The weather can turn warm and sunny during the month of January, inviting one to explore the quiet woods and fields. The first flowers to bloom are very much appreciated, giving us an early glimpse of the coming pageantry of spring. As the storms return, it's time to venture out onto the windswept coastal bluffs or into the great stillness of the redwood forests, for in these magical places you will find the essence of Mendocino County on a winter day.

## (1) Fetid Adder's Tongue – Slink Pod *(Scoliopus bigelovii)*, 2×A/S

**When:** Fetid Adder's Tongue is one of the very first wildflowers of the New Year. The blooming cycle may start during the second week in January and continue into early March (Jan.– March).

**Where:** Slink Pod is found near the coast in moist forests of redwood, tan oak, and white fir. My wife and I look for the first *S. bigelovii* in such areas as Faulkner County Park and along the shaded banks of Orr Springs Road west of Comptche. Some of the most impressive leaves and flowers of Fetid Adder's Tongue are found inland from the coast, along the banks of Highway 1 east of Rockport.

**What:** *S. bigelovii* is a member of the Lily family. The mottled, shiny green leaves are up to twelve inches long, and as many as nine flowers may grow from the center of the plant. After the flowers are gone, a small seed pod, resembling a beechnut, forms at the end of each eight-to-ten-inch stem, causing the plant to droop, or slink, thus "Slink Pod." Be fore-warned— unfortunately, these exotic-looking plants have an unpleasant odor.

## (2) Manzanita Flowers *(Arctostaphylos sp.)*, A/S

**When:** The flowers of some species of Manzanita bloom about mid-January (Jan.– May).

**Where:** *Arctostaphylos sp.* is found in all parts of the county, from the coast to the high country of the inner mountains. You'll find the earliest-blooming species of *Arctostaphylos* at lower elevations, from the coast to the inner valley foothills and woodlands.

**What:** Manzanita is a member of the heath family, with at least fifteen species in Mendocino County. Manzanita shrubs growing in the foothills are particularly lovely during or after a rainstorm. The dark reddish-brown branches and trunk glis-ten, casting the entire plant into beautiful shades of mahogany. The flowers are urn-shaped and may be either white or pink.

## (3) Milk Maids – Rain Bells – Spring Beauty *(Cardamine californica)*, A/S

**When:** The early blossoms of Milk Maids will appear by the third or fourth week of January (Jan.– April).

**Where:** Rain Bells enjoy the sheltered woods of our foothills and forests from the coast to the inner mountains. We look for the first Rain Bells in the wooded foothills on the northeast side of Lake Mendocino.

**What:** Spring Beauty is a member of the Mustard family, and one of the earliest wildflowers of the year. The flowers vary from white to pink, growing in loose clusters. Two differently shaped leaves accompany each plant: rounded leaves at the base of the stem, and three-fingered leaves opposite the flower clusters.

## (4) Coast Silk Tassel Tree *(Garrya elliptica)*, ½ A/S

**When:** The lovely catkins of the Coast Silk Tassel Tree may be seen during early to mid-January (Jan.– March).

**Where:** The species *G. elliptica* is found directly along the coast. Beautiful specimens thrive between Gualala and the coastal town of Elk, particularly in the Elk Creek basin several miles south of town.

**What:** A member of the Silk Tassel family, *G. elliptica* will reach the height of a small tree. When in full bloom, *G. elliptica* is draped with a magnificent mantle of small yellowish flowers, strung together like beads hung in an elegant entryway.

# JANUARY

**(1) Fetid Adder's Tongue**

**(2) Manzanita Flowers**

**(3) Milk Maids**

**(4) Coast Silk Tassel Tree**

# FEBRUARY

Storm clouds roll in from the coast, carrying winter rains that seem to never let up; the wet season has settled in for a February visit. The dark sky drips moisture day and night, hiding the sun in a cloak of gray. Suddenly the rain ends, the sun breaks through, and the wet fields and meadows start to dry, great clouds of steam rising into the clean shimmering air. Within a day the weather has turned toward early spring, wildflowers showing bits of color against the greening countryside. Deep in the redwoods, water from the heavy rains carves small streams that run to the rivers, then to the ocean. The lovely Manzanita's urn-shaped flowers paint the hillsides with color, and along the canyon streams, the yellow bloom of the Pepperwood trees scents the air. A walk in the openings of the wooded foothills tells you that the Shooting Stars and Indian Warriors have begun their journey. The long rains and occasional sunny days of February provide time for solitude and reflection, a time for restful walks through the quiet winter scenery of Mendocino County.

## (5) Shooting Stars – Johnny Jump-Up *(Dodecatheon hendersonii)*, A / S +

**When:** Shooting Stars start their blooming cycle during early February (Feb.–April).

**Where:** Johnny Jump-Up grows in grassy, shaded wooded areas from the coast to the inner mountain range. Because we live in Ukiah we look for the first Johnny Jump-Ups in the wooded foothills of Low Gap County Park and at Lake Mendocino.

**What:** *D. hendersonii* is a lovely member of the Primrose family. When you find the first Shooting Stars, rejoice—they are the harbingers of spring.

## (6) Pepperwood Tree – California Bay *(Umbellularia californica)*, A / S

**When:** Pepperwood trees display their clusters of yellow flowers by late February (Feb.–April).

**Where:** California Bay is found on semi-open hillsides and fields, and on the edges of our redwood forests. The Bay tree roots in deep forests along the banks of streams where enough light can penetrate the forest canopy. Many beautiful Pepperwood trees grow along Orr Springs Road and Highway 128 to the coast.

**What:** The California Bay tree is a member of the Laurel family. Although it grows as a solitary tree, the finest examples are found when it forms groves of more than five trees. I found a special grove where more than seven trees had formed a hidden glen, ten yards long, shielded from sight. From a distance the trees appeared as one. The leaves of the Bay tree have a pungent, spicy scent that delights me and will always remind me of Mendocino County.

## (7) Indian Warriors – Yellow *(Pedicularis densiflora)*, ½ A / S

**Where:** In all the years my wife and I have looked for wildflowers, we've seen only four or five yellow Indian Warriors. I'm sure there are more. We found several plants on the north side of Lake Mendocino and a few in Montgomery Woods State Reserve.

## (8) Indian Warriors *(Pedicularis densiflora)*, ½ A / S

**When:** You'll find the early bloom of the delicate, fern-like flower bracts of Indian Warriors in late January; surely by the first week in February (Feb.–April).

**Where:** *P. densiflora* is found throughout the county in mixed evergreen forests and shaded woodlands, and along many of our back roads. Almost any of the roads in wooded areas—Orr Springs Road, Mountain View Road, or Low Gap Road—are prime places to enjoy these plants. A great stand of Indian Warriors remains intact in a wooded area on the campus of Mendocino Community College.

**What:** A member of the Figwort family, Indian Warriors grow in colonies that stand as quiet sentinels, awaiting the approaching spring. The beautiful reddish color of the flowers, and the green fern fronds, carpet many road banks and forest openings, making this plant one of my favorites.

**(5) Shooting Stars**

**(6) Pepperwood Tree**

**(7) & (8) Indian Warriors**

## (9) Baby Blue Eyes (Nemophila menziesii), A/S

**When:** The early bloom of Baby Blue Eyes is mid-February (Feb.–April).

**Where:** *N. menziesii* is found from the coastal headlands to the inner valleys, open meadows and fields, and grass-covered hills. The early parts of Orr Springs Road west of Ukiah, and Route 162 east of Covelo, have beautiful displays of Baby Blue Eyes. Some of the largest flowers of *N. menziesii* are found on the coastal headlands north of Fort Bragg.

**What:** A member of the Waterleaf family, Baby Blue Eyes may be the best known and loved of all our wildflowers. When the delicate, bright to pale-blue flowers are in mass, hillsides and meadows shimmer with their lovely color.

## (10) Scarlet Larkspur (Delphinium nudicaule), A/S

**When:** You'll notice the first bloom of Scarlet Larkspur by late February or early March (Feb.–April).

**Where:** Scarlet Larkspur thrives both in open shade and full sun on the moist hillsides of many of our back roads. Outstanding displays of Scarlet Larkspur are found on such roads as Orr Springs and Mill Creek Canyon.

**What:** *D. nudicaule* is a member of the Buttercup family. When found on open rocky side hills, Scarlet Larkspur produces dense hues of orange-red, resembling color patterns painted by a master impressionist.

## (11) Coltsfoot (Petasites palmatus), ½ A/S

**When:** The first Coltsfoot blooms by the end of February (Feb.–April).

**Where:** Coltsfoot is found from the coast inland, in moist wooded areas near streams and seeps. Large colonies thrive along such roads as Flynn Creek and Comptche–Mendocino.

**What:** Coltsfoot is a member of the Aster family. The flower head forms clusters of white-to-pinkish flowers supported by a thick stem with large, rounded lobed leaves. *P. palmatus* lends a sense of grace and order to the roadside seeps and hidden forest glens that it inhabits.

## (12) Hound's Tongue (Cynoglossum grande), A/S +

**When:** The leaves of Hound's Tongue are noticed first; clusters of blue flowers soon follow by early March (Feb.–April).

**Where:** Hound's Tongue is found in moist wooded foothills from the coast to the inner mountain range. Back roads such as Mountain View Road and Orr Springs Road are peaceful areas for viewing the lovely blue flowers of Hound's Tongue.

**What:** *C. grande* is a member of the Borage family. Hound's Tongue is so called because the leaves are said to resemble a hound's tongue. The plant may reach a height of two feet, with a panicle of loosely clustered flowers showing pink and then turning bright blue after fertilization.

# FEBRUARY

**(9) Baby Blue Eyes**

**(10) Scarlet Larkspur**

**(11) Coltsfoot**

**(12) Hound's Tongue**

## (13) Manzanita Flowers *(Arctostaphylos canescens ssp. canescens)*, A/S +

**When:** Because a number of different species of Manzanita grow in the county, it's difficult to pick an exact time for flower bloom. Most of the Manzanita bloom from January into April. The Manzanita species *A. canescens* will flower by mid-February (Jan.–April).

**Where:** *A. canescens* is found from the coast to the inner mountains, and is commonly seen on many of our back roads, including Low Gap County Park and Mountain View Road.

**What:** A member of the Heath family, *A. canescens* is a beautiful shrub with pale-green leaves that, under certain lighting conditions, take on a truly remarkable silvery gray color.

## (14) Blue Blossom *(Ceanothus thyrsiflorus)*, A/S

**When:** The early bloom of *C. thyrsiflorus* appears on the coast by early February (Feb.–June).

**Where:** *C. thyrsiflorus* is found west of Highway 101 to the coast. The more conspicuous shrubs hug the coastal headlands. Fine examples of Blue Blossom grow south of Elk on Highway 1. In the 1960s, when my family traveled to the coast on Orr Springs Road, we noticed large masses of Blue Blossom thriving in the logged redwood forests.

**What:** Blue Blossom is a member of the Buckthorn family. *C. thyrsiflorus* appears twice in this book. The photograph on the opposite page is representative of the windswept coastal version that grows along the ocean bluffs.

## (15) Valerian *(Valeriana sitchensis ssp. scouleri)*, A/S +

**When:** Valerian blooms by late February (Feb.–April).

**Where:** *V. sitchensis* grows in a very limited area along the coast, on moist, shaded road banks. My wife and I find it blooming next to Highway 1 in the Elk Creek basin south of Elk.

**What:** *V. sitchensis* is a member of the Valerian family. Rare in Mendocino County, the species becomes more plentiful as you travel north into British Columbia. Valerian has a semi-rounded head with small tubular flowers that are a lovely shade of pink and white.

## (16) Gorse *(Ulex europaeus)*, 1/10 A/S

**When:** Gorse has a long blooming cycle that starts in early February and lasts into late June (Feb.–June).

**Where:** Often mistaken for Scotch Broom, Gorse is found on the coast in fields and meadows, with the largest concentrations near the town of Caspar.

**What:** This weedy non-native shrub is a member of the Pea family. From a distance, Gorse is quite attractive, growing in large masses and producing a rich yellow hue that blends with the seascape. Beware: *U. europaeus* forms impenetrable thickets of dense branches covered with sharp one-to-two-inch spines that will literally rip the clothes off your back. I've watched people use bulldozers to remove large masses of Gorse to make room for a house lot, only to find that within a year or two it's back with a vengeance.

**(13) Manzanita Flowers**

**(14) Blue Blossom**

**(15) Valerian**

**(16) Gorse**

MARCH

The month of March is the color green in Mendocino County. The color of the meadows and hills takes on a startling green mantle that must, I am sure, parallel that of the Emerald Isle. After summer's long heat and the wet darkness of early winter, it seems as though Nature has done the impossible: she has produced hillside palettes of color, mixing rain and seed into the earth to repaint the dreary gray landscape in lovely shades of green.

## (17) Poppy *(Eschscholzia californica)*, ½ A/S

**When:** You'll see early signs of our beautiful California Poppy by mid-March. The blooming cycle continues into August and beyond (March–Oct.).

**Where:** The California Poppy is one of our loveliest wildflowers, and may be seen on most county roads. The poppies of Mendocino County inhabit open fields and meadows from the coast to the inner valleys and mountains. Beautiful displays of *E. californica* are found in such areas as Round Valley and the coastal headlands near Manchester.

**What:** Viewing the California coastline from their ships, early Spanish sailors called it "The land of fire," because the coastal hills and headlands were aflame with the color yellow. A member of the poppy family, *E. californica* has been cultivated throughout the world.

## (18) Goldfields *(Lasthenia californica)*, 2 × A/S

**When:** The first glimpse of the small yellow Goldfields occurs in late February; their numbers will be more noticeable mid-March (Feb.–April).

**Where:** The close-cropped side hills and thin rocky topsoil of our open fields produce the best viewing of these colorful flowers. Driving on our inland valley back roads, you'll see great masses of Goldfields on the hills, which, from a distance, appear to be smeared with butter. The yellow hue against the green rolling hills of the countryside is a remarkable contrast in color and beauty.

**What:** Goldfields are a member of the Sunflower family.

## (19) Common Meadow Foam *(Limnanthes douglasii ssp. nivea)*, A/S

**When:** The first patches of Meadow Foam will be noticeable in late February. March and April are usually the best months for viewing the lavish showing of these lovely flowers (Feb.–April).

**Where:** The white-to-yellowish flowers of *L. douglasii* are found along many of our back roads and in valleys and open hillside meadows throughout the county. The Willits Valley and the Toll Road east of Hopland provide excellent viewing of Meadow Foam.

**What:** *Limnanthes* is a member of the Meadowfoam family. The flowers are so densely packed and tumbled together that they resemble the foam of an ocean wave as it retreats from a sandy beach.

## (20) Western Buttercup *(Ranunculus occidentalis)*, A/S

**When:** The first Buttercups may appear in small, scattered groups in late February, but by the end of March you'll start to notice them in larger concentrations (Feb.–May).

**Where:** Western Buttercup is found in grassy meadows, fields, and wooded side hills on almost all of our back roads. The Toll Road east of Hopland, as it starts its upward climb through the grassy oak-covered hills, offers magnificent displays of Buttercup.

**What:** *R. occidentalis* is a member of the Buttercup family. When Buttercups are seen clustered on wooded side hills or in open meadows, the show is spectacular, especially when back-lit by early morning or late evening light.

**(18) Goldfields**

**(17) Poppy**

**(19) Common Meadow Foam**

**(20) Western Buttercup**

## (21) Windflower – Wood Anemone *(Anemone oregana)*, A / S

**When:** Windflowers may show their first delicate bloom by late February; but the best time to look will be during early March (March – May).

**Where:** For the gentle Windflower, the best viewing is in the mixed forests and redwoods west of Highway 101 to the coast. While walking in the shade of a forest glen some quiet morning, you'll happen upon a bed of Windflowers that seems to stir with just the faintest whisper of a breeze. We seek and find the shy Wood Anemone along the banks of Orr Springs Road, in Montgomery Woods State Reserve, and in Hendy Woods State Park.

**What:** The dainty white or pink-tinged flowers of *A. oregana* are members of the Buttercup family.

## (22) False Solomon's Seal *(Smilacina racemosa)*, ¼ A / S

**When:** You'll see the first flowers of *S. recemosa* blooming by mid-March (March – April).

**Where:** False Solomon's Seal is found in partially shaded woodlands from the coast to the inner mountain range. Driving along the coast on Highway 1 or inland on back roads like Orr Springs Road will reward you with beautiful displays of *S. racemosa*.

**What:** Solomon's Seal is a member of the Lily family. When they first bloom, the flowers are a yellow cream color that turns white as they age. The beautiful, shiny red color of the berries is well worth a look in the late summer and early fall.

## (23) Snow Queen – Kittentails *(Synthyris reniformis)*, ½ A / S

**When:** Snow Queen, also called Kittentails, first appears in early March (March – April).

**Where:** Kittentails relish the moist shaded redwoods and forests west of Highway 101 to the coast. They thrive in the understory of the evergreen forest along Orr Springs Road in Montgomery Woods State Reserve.

**What:** A member of the Figwort family, Snow Queen has lovely, deep-green heart-shaped leaves with toothed margins. Set above the attractive leaves, the small, loosely branched clusters of pink-to-white bell-shaped flowers add charm and beauty to any forest setting.

## (24) Skunk Cabbage *(Lysichitum americanum)*, ½ A / S

**When:** The lavish green leaves of Skunk Cabbage are apparent in late February; by March, a ten-inch green spike covered with tiny yellowish flowers will appear, giving a tropical look to the plant and its surroundings (March – May).

**Where:** Skunk Cabbage likes wet coastal swamps and bogs. Look for Skunk Cabbage, with its huge oblong leaves, near marshy creeks and streams that empty into the ocean at locations such as Elk Creek basin and Russian Gulch State Park.

**What:** This strange, exotic-looking plant belongs in the Arum family, and may be found as far north as Alaska.

# MARCH

**(21) Windflower**

**(22) False Solomon's Seal**

**(23) Snow Queen**

**(24) Skunk Cabbage**

**(25) A bed of five Red Trilliums,** ¼ A/S

**(26) Red Trillium,** A/S

**(27) White Trillium,** A/S

**(28) A bed of five White Trilliums,** ¼ A/S

## Trillium – Giant Trillium *(Trillium chloropetalum)*.

**When:** *T. chloropetalum* will first show signs of blooming toward mid-March. Depending on elevation and habitat, the blooming cycle for Giant Trillium may last through April (March–May).

**Where:** *T. chloropetalum* is found sparsely from the coast to the inner mountains. Giant Trillium prefers wooded canyons near streams and creeks, and partially open woods and brush. I have most luck finding Giant Trillium in the foothills east of Highway 101. My wife and I always look for the first white Trillium of the year in Mill Creek Canyon east of Ukiah. We've seen the red variety growing east of Hopland, on the Old Toll Road near the Sheldon Creek campground. We located several groups of more than five plants blooming on the Lake County side of the Toll Road.

**What:** Trillium, also referred to as the Giant Trillium, is a member of the Lily family. It will grow to two feet in height, with its three-petaled flower standing above three large oval-shaped leaves. The green leaves have distinctive purple blotches that mark them with one of Nature's secret codes. The flowers have a heavy fragrance, reminiscent of the deep woods and hidden places Trilliums inhabit.

**Note:** The images of the Red Trillium on the opposite page were taken in 1990 on the Toll Road east of Hopland. My wife and I have visited this place over the years, watching delightedly as the little stand of trillium came back year after year. Late in March 1997, I visited this special place once more, to see how the small group was doing. Much to my sorrow, I found that some misguided person or persons had dug them up. I can only hope they might be surviving in some private garden.

# MARCH

**(25) A bed of five Red Trilliums**

**(26) Red Trillium**

**(27) White Trillium**

**(28) A bed of five White Trilliums**

## (29) Indian Paintbrush *(Castilleja foliolosa)*, A/S

**When:** There are seven or eight species of Indian Paintbrush that grow in Mendocino County. The early foothill species, *C. foliolosa* will bloom in March, while other species will bloom during the spring and summer months (March–Aug.).

**Where:** The genus *Castilleja* blooms on the coastal headlands, rocky hillsides and cliffs, along our back roads, and inland in the wooded foothills and high mountains of our inner coastal range. The photograph of *C. foliolosa* on the opposite page was taken on a rocky hillside on Orr Springs Road in March 1997. You'll also find *C. foliolosa* blooming in early March on the Old Toll Road east of Hopland.

**What:** Indian Paintbrush belongs to the Figwort family, and is among our most recognized wildflowers. The color of the various species may run from orange-yellow to deep red. Clusters of paintbrush can be seen blooming high on rocky canyon walls, reflecting astonishing colors. You'll marvel at the severe environment paintbrush choose to inhabit, and wonder how they got there and how they survive.

## (30) Lupine *(Lupinus sp.)*, A/S

**When:** Lovely lupine shows off its elegant colors with great style. We see the first flowers of our early Lupine species by mid-March (March–July).

**Where:** Lupine forms great masses of color on road banks, hillsides and coastal bluffs, and in open fields and meadows. Its beautiful flowers are seen throughout Mendocino County.

**What:** At least twenty species of Lupine grow within Mendocino County's borders. A member of the Pea family, *Lupinus sp.* adds much color and enjoyment to the countryside during our spring and early summer months.

## (31) Iris – Ground Iris *(Iris macrosiphon)*, A/S

**When:** *I. macrosiphon* presents itself by mid-March, and continues to bloom in diverse regions of the county well into May (March–May).

**Where:** Ground Iris is found in semi-shaded foothills, on grassy road banks, and in the forests of the inner coastal range. Many lovely specimens of Ground Iris are found on such back roads as Orr Springs Road and Low Gap Road.

**What:** *I. macrosiphon* belongs to the Iris family. At least half a dozen species of Iris grow in the county, varying in color from white to deep purple. *I. macrosiphon* grows individually, or in clusters forming carpets of brilliant blue-to-purple against the grassy hillsides and wooded foothills.

## (32) Popcorn Flower *(Plagiobothrys nothofulvus)*, 2 × A/S

**When:** The first Popcorn flowers appear in late March (March–May).

**Where:** Common in our county, Popcorn flowers are seen along most of our back roads, in grassy fields, and on open slopes. Mountain House Road and Low Gap Road have fine displays of Popcorn Flowers.

**What:** *P. nothofulvus* is a member of the Borage family. The small popcorn-like flowers are coiled on stems one to two feet tall. Seen from a distance, fields of Popcorn Flowers appear as numerous specks of white, as though a late-winter storm had paid a visit to a hillside meadow.

# MARCH

**(29) Indian Paintbrush**

**(30) Lupine**

**(31) Iris**

**(32) Popcorn Flower**

## (33) Pink Flowering Currant *(Ribes sanguineum var. glutinosum)*, ½ A/S

**When:** Wild Currant, a tree-like shrub, sends forth its beautiful clusters of pink blossoms by mid-March (March–April).

**Where:** *R. sanguineum* likes the moist coastal woodlands on or near the coast. Handsome displays of Wild Currant are found on many of our back roads near the coast, such as the Branscomb Road and Orr Springs Road. My wife and I enjoy parking outside the entrance to the Caspar Cemetery and walking up the road to look for Flowering Currant and other wildflowers that grow in this forest sanctuary.

**What:** Flowering currant is a member of the Gooseberry family. The clusters of flowers show jewel-like elegance, reflecting their lovely pink color in the forest darkness. The flowers have a subtle fragrance that permeates the stillness of the woods, leaving one with a sense of contentment.

## (34) Wild Ginger – Long-tailed Ginger *(Asarum caudatum)*, A/S

**When:** The handsome Wild Ginger leaves are in evidence all year. The dark-brown flowers bloom from March through May (March–May).

**Where:** Look for Wild Ginger along creeks and streams, and in the moist forests of both the coastal redwoods and the wooded canyons east of Highway 101.

Beautiful specimens of Wild Ginger may be found on Orr Springs Road west of Comptche, and east of Ukiah in the Mill Creek Canyon above the dams.

**What:** *A. caudatum* belongs to the Pipevine family. The exotic reddish-brown flowers, shaped like some small forest creature, lie mostly hidden under the kidney-shaped green leaves, which when crushed give off the distinctive smell of ginger.

## (35) Redwood Sorrel *(Oxalis oregana)*, A/S

**When:** The flowers of *O. oregana* bloom in late February (Feb.–May).

**Where:** The lovely pink flowers of Redwood Sorrel are found in the redwoods on the shaded forest floor from the coast inland. Roads that follow the redwoods, such as Highway 128 and Orr Springs Road, and areas such as Hendy Woods State Park, are excellent places to find *O. oregana*.

**What:** A member of the Oxalis family, the leaves of Redwood Sorrel look very much like clover leaves. The beautiful carpets of Redwood Sorrel, one of Nature's wild gardens, add elegance and color to the forest settings where it grows.

## (36) Salmonberry Flower *(Rubus spectabilis)*, A/S

**When:** The rose-like flowers of Salmonberry bloom in early March (March–May).

**Where:** You'll find the Salmonberry shrub in the cool coastal canyons and seeps that lead to the ocean. Roads such as Highway 1 from the coast inland, and areas such as Russian Gulch State Park, allow for leisurely exploration while you look for *R. spectabilis* and other coastal plants.

**What:** Salmonberry shrub is a member of the Rose family. In late spring, when the rose-colored flower petals drop, the fruit soon appears in the shape of beautiful berries the color of glistening salmon eggs. Salmonberry leaves are of the lightest green; with the bright-pink flowers, the effect is most pleasing against the dark background of the coastal woods.

# MARCH

**(34) Wild Ginger**

**(33) Pink Flowering Currant**

**(35) Redwood Sorrel**

**(36) Salmonberry Flower**

## (37) Purple Mouse Ears *(Mimulus douglasii)*, 2 × A/S

**When:** Purple Mouse Ears bloom by mid-March, and their colorful flower display lasts well into April (March–May).

**Where:** *M. douglasii* is uncommon in the county. We look for it on the thin soil of dirt banks and rocky open meadows. Look for Purple Mouse Ears on Fish Rock Road, the county road to Lake Pillsbury, and Snow Mountain west of Hopland.

**What:** The flower head of this delightful little plant is smaller than a dime and stands only one to two inches tall. One of the smallest members of the Figwort family, it will occasionally find company with the Kellogg's Monkey Flower.

## (38) Kellogg's Monkey Flower *(Mimulus kelloggii)*, A/S

**When:** The first Kellogg's Monkey Flower will bloom near the end of March (March–May).

**Where:** My wife and I find these small rose-colored wildflowers growing in thin rocky soil on open road banks and meadows. *M. kelloggii* is fairly common in the county, mostly east of Highway 101. We find the colorful *M. kelloggii* blooming on the county road to Lake Pillsbury, on Mill Creek Road, and, in late June, on a gravel flat near the summit of Anthony Peak.

**What:** The Kellogg's Monkey Flower is a member of the Figwort family. When growing in large concentrations, *M. kelloggii* presents a feast of color that's hard to duplicate in any private garden.

## (39) Blue-eyed Mary *(Collinsia sparsiflora var. arvensis)*, 2 × A/S

**When:** Blue-eyed Mary's colorful bloom is usually in evidence by the second week in March (March–May).

**Where:** Mainly a plant of Mendocino County's interior valleys, Collinsia is found on open grassy hillside banks and on shaded wooded foothills. *C. sparsiflora* enjoys the rocky, grassy soil in areas like Low Gap County Park and the old Hopland–Yorkville Road west of Hopland.

**What:** A member of the Figwort family, *C. sparsiflora* is one of several species found in our county. Blue-eyed Mary is a delightful plant to find and observe, rewarding you with its delicately shaped flower and sublime color.

## (40) Lace Pod *(Thysanocarpus curvipes var. elegans)*, A/S +

**When:** The first small pods of *T. curvipes* may be seen by early March (March–June).

**Where:** Lace Pod is found in grassy open fields and semi-wooded foothills in such areas as Low Gap County Park and Route 162 leading into Round Valley.

**What:** A member of the Mustard family, Lace Pod should not be overlooked while hiking the meadows and hillsides. When back-lit by the sun, the seed-like pods are beautiful in shape and design, reflecting the work of a master craftsman.

# MARCH

**(37) Purple Mouse Ears**

**(38) Kellogg's Monkey Flower**

**(39) Blue-eyed Mary**

**(40) Lace Pod**

## (41) Pink Fawn Lily (Erythronium revolutum), A/S

**When:** *E. revolutum* usually blooms by the third week in March (March–April).

**Where:** In all the years we have been looking at wildflowers, we've seen the Pink Fawn Lily in only two locations. If found at all, it grows near the coast, in wet soil near creeks and streams and in shaded open woods. The photograph on the opposite page, taken in 1992, is of one of seven plants growing on a shaded road bank near Comptche.

**What:** In Mendocino County, *E. revolutum* is rare and endangered. The light-to-deep shade of pink reflected from the petals, and the yellow markings inside the base, make this member of the Lily family a special gift from Nature. Apparently, this species of *Erythronium* is more common in Oregon, Mendocino County being at the southern end of its range. Hopefully, you'll find this rare treasure on one of your wildflower journeys.

## (42) Yellow Monkey Flower (Mimulus guttatus), A/S +

**When:** You'll see the first yellow monkey flowers blooming by late March or early April (March–July).

**Where:** *M. guttatus* blooms throughout the county, from the coast to the inner mountains, enjoying moist habitats near seeps and springs. The photograph on the opposite page represents a single flower isolated from a large array of Monkey Flowers growing near a seep on Orr Springs Road.

**What:** Yellow Monkey Flower is a member of the Figwort family. *M. guttatus* offers many variations in size, depending upon where in the county it grows.

## (43) Miner's Lettuce (Claytonia perfoliata ssp. perfoliata), A/S

**When:** Miner's Lettuce leaves and their tiny white flowers bloom by early March (March–June).

**Where:** You'll find Miner's lettuce growing in almost every nook and cranny of Mendocino County. Some of the most robust plants may be found in moist shaded hillsides near seeps and streams. Coastal locations like Russian Gulch State Park, and inland areas such as Low Gap County Park, are excellent places to see these interesting plants.

**What:** A member of the Purslane family, Miner's Lettuce has long been used in England as a garnish for salads. Early Native Americans scattered the leaves of the plant near anthills, allowing the ants to crawl over the lettuce, which gave it a somewhat vinegar-like sour taste.

## (44) Coastal Fairy Bells (Disporum smithii), ½ A/S

**When:** Coastal Fairy Bells will bloom by mid-March (March–May).

**Where:** *D. smithii* likes cool canyons and shady forests on or near the coast. My wife and I like to explore the road leading into the Caspar Cemetery for the shy, hidden Fairy Bells and the other wildflowers that inhabit this quiet place.

**What:** Coastal Fairy Bells are members of the Lily family. The small plant has branching stems with beautiful, oval-shaped, lightly veined leaves. As you walk in the moist woods you must be patient with Fairy Bells. You bend and stoop, and finally peer under some foliage, and as if by magic, a cluster of whitish bell-shaped flowers is revealed, suspended from beneath two lovely leaves.

# MARCH

**(41) Pink Fawn Lily**

**(42) Yellow Monkey Flower**

**(43) Miner's Lettuce**

**(44) Coastal Fairy Bells**

## (45) Cream Fawn Lilies – Easter Lily *(Erythronium californicum)*, ½ A / S

**When:** The delicate flowers of the Easter Lily start to bloom in late February or early March (March–April).

**Where:** Cream Fawn Lilies, also called Easter Lilies, are found blooming in the moist woods and foothills, and along the sides of many of our back roads both near the coast and inland. On Orr Springs Road we counted more than 100 plants blooming on a sunny, open side hill. The beautifully shaped Fawn Lilies are always a treat to see. Their quiet coloring and graceful appearance add a touch of richness and grace to any landscape where they choose to grow.

**What:** Easter Lily is a member of the Lily family. The green leaves are slightly mottled and stand erect, showcasing the beautiful cream-colored hue of the petals and the yellow markings inside the throat.

## (46) Calypso – Redwood Orchid – Fairy Slipper *(Calypso bulbosa)*, 2 × A / S

**When:** You'll find a few Redwood Orchids in bloom by the end of February, but the best time to look is during the second week in March (Feb.–April).

**Where:** We usually look for the small, delicate Calypso flowers toward the coast, in mixed forests of redwoods, fir, and hardwoods; however, they are also found inland in the dense woods of areas like Pine Ridge Road east of Willits. Be careful where you step while walking in the deep forest: Calypso flowers are small and difficult to see. My wife and I enjoy looking for them in Montgomery Woods State Reserve. *C. bulbosa* is found in the northern parts of both the East and West Coasts, ranging as far north as Alaska and east into Siberia.

**What:** Fairy Slipper is a member of the Orchid family. First you'll see a single oval-shaped leaf lying on the forest floor. Soon after, the dainty orchid-shaped flower will appear, supported on a stem four to six inches tall. While walking in Montgomery Woods State Reserve, I counted more than twenty plants growing from a hollow, moss-covered log. If you sit quietly in a forest setting, perhaps realization of what Nature has accomplished will come to you when you see the giant redwoods guarding these fairy-like flowers.

## (47) Wake Robin *(Trillium ovatum)*, ½ A / S

**When:** The first flowers of *T. ovatum* appear toward the end of February, certainly by the first week of March (Feb.–April).

**Where:** The Wake Robin loves the moist forest floors of our coastal redwoods, and the mixed forests west of Highway 101. You'll find Wake Robins growing on the banks of many of the back roads that approach the coast. Quiet places to enjoy *T. ovatum* include Hendy Woods State Park, Montgomery Woods State Reserve, and along Route 128 in the redwoods leading coastward.

**What:** The lovely Wake Robin is a member of the Lily family. The three petals of the flower stand above a whorl of three leaves. When walking in the dark woods on some cold, wet winter day, the beautiful white of the petals will spark your eye, telling you that spring will soon be here.

## (48) Calypso Orchid and Leaf *(Calypso bulbosa)*, ½ A / S

**What:** On the opposite page, the photograph of a Calypso Orchid and its one leaf might give you an indication of its relative size and habitat.

# MARCH

**(45) Cream Fawn Lilies**

**(46) Calypso**

**(47) Wake Robin**

**(48) Calypso Orchid and Leaf**

## (49) Mission Bells (Fritillaria lanceolata), A/S

**When:** The very first Mission Bells start to bloom toward the end of February. In different parts of the county the cycle of bloom lasts into late April (Feb.–April).

**Where:** Mission Bells may be found in shaded woodlands and foothills from the coast to the inner mountain ranges. Coastal regions like Elk Creek basin on Highway 1, and inland in areas like Low Gap County Park and the shaded banks of Orr Springs Road and Mill Creek Road, are excellent places to find the lovely *F. lanceolata*.

**What:** Members of the Lily family, Mission Bells are aptly named because of their bell-shaped flowers. The blossoms are suspended one above the other, as though waiting for the slightest breeze to ring in the coming spring. The color of the petals may vary from pale yellow to dark brown. In Mill Creek canyon we found a plant with nine flowers hanging from a stalk nearly three feet tall.

## (50) Flowering Gooseberry (Ribes californicum var. californicum), 2 × A/S

**When:** *R. californicum* starts to show its beautiful fuchsia-shaped flowers by the end of February, and will be in full bloom by mid-March (Feb.–April).

**Where:** One of several species found growing throughout the county, Flowering Gooseberry, also called Hillside Gooseberry, likes partially open side hills, wooded areas, and some of our steeper brushy canyons. I particularly like the Toll Road east of old Hopland, and Fish Rock Road south of Boonville to the coast, for some of the finest specimens of this native shrub.

**What:** *Ribes californicum*, a member of the Gooseberry family, is a medium-sized plant with a dense, extremely thorny branch structure. Flowering Gooseberry is a marvelous sight in full bloom. The entire plant becomes dotted with intricate flowers that will make you pause in a woodland setting for a closer look.

## (51) Blue Dicks (Dichelostemma capitatum ssp. capitatum), A/S

**When:** The colorful blue-violet flowers of Blue Dicks start their first bloom by late February. The blooming cycle may last into early May (Feb.–April).

**Where:** *D. capitatum* is found in the open meadows and hills of our inner valleys. Blue Dicks are quite noticeable along the sides of such back roads as Orr Springs Road and Mountain House Road. I always feel an enjoyable sense of continuity when I find the early bloom of these lovely flowers.

**What:** Blue Dicks are a member of the Lily family, and are the early bloomers among several more species of *Dichelostemma* that bloom later in the spring and early summer. The flower head consists of a congested group of tiny blue-violet flowers resting at the top of an eight-to-eighteen-inch tubular stem.

## (52) Claytonia (Claytonia parviflora ssp. parviflora), A/S

**When:** Claytonia may flower in early March; however, by late March and early April, the lovely magenta-colored flowers will be in full bloom (March–May).

**Where:** Claytonia is found in wooded foothills and shaded road banks inland from the coast. A rocky serpentine bank near Soda Creek, on Route 128 between Yorkville and Boonville, offers a lovely display of colorful Claytonia flowers.

**What:** Claytonia is a member of the Purslane family. The small lavender-striped flowers are found growing in masses, producing an elegant magenta hue rarely seen in the wildflower color spectrum. Another species of Claytonia, *Claytonia gypsophiloides*, is very similar in appearance, showing little difference to the casual viewer.

# MARCH

**(49) Mission Bells**

**(50) Flowering Gooseberry**

**(51) Blue Dicks**

**(52) Claytonia**

## (53) Mertens Saxifrage *(Saxifraga mertensiana)*, ¾ A/S

**When:** Mertens Saxifrage starts blooming during the early March (March–May).

**Where:** *S. mertensiana* is quite common, and can be found in semi-shaded mixed forests, growing on grassy hillsides near creeks and streams and on moss-covered rocks. Orr Creek in Low Gap County Park, and Orr Springs Road in Montgomery Woods State Reserve, are excellent areas to find Mertens Saxifrage, which ranges from Sonoma County north through Oregon and Washington into Alaska.

**What:** Mertens Saxifrage is a member of the Saxifrage family. The green leaves are rounded and lobed, and lie flat on moss-covered rocks and grassy banks. The small white flowers, with narrow petals, are suspended above the leaves on stems up to twelve inches tall.

## (54) Cream Cup *(Platystemon californicus)*, ¾ A/S

**When:** The first Cream Cups arrive by mid-March; by early April they are in full bloom, lasting well into May (March–June).

**Where:** Cream Cups enjoy the coastal headlands and the wet meadows and hills of the inner valleys; they also do well on thin soil and serpentine rock. The headlands north of Fort Bragg and Pudding Creek produce large masses of Cream Cups that are outstanding in color and size. Other areas where Cream Cups do well are Eastside Road and Low Gap County Park.

**What:** Cream Cups are members of the Poppy family. On close examination you'll notice that each cream-colored petal is marked in soft yellow at the tip. In April, small areas of coastal meadows turn creamy yellow from the color of *P. californicus*, adding to the already beautiful colors of early spring.

## (55) Sun Cups – Cowslips *(Camissonia ovata)*, A/S +

**When:** By mid-March the first Sun Cups, also called Cowslips, will be in bloom (March–May).

**Where:** You'll find Sun Cups creating small scattered patches of brilliant yellow on grassy side hills and meadows. Look for Cowslips in such areas as Low Gap County Park, and along Highway 101 between Hopland and Ukiah.

**What:** Sun Cups belong to the Evening Primrose family. The leaves lie flat on the ground, at first glance resembling Dandelion leaves. The flowers are positioned toward the center, where the axil of the leaf is formed. One plant may have as many as ten flowers. The apparent flower stem is actually a calyx tube, with the seed buried just beneath the ground.

## (56) California Saxifrage *(Saxifraga californica)*, A/S

**When:** You'll notice the first bloom of California Saxifrage in early March (March–May).

**Where:** California Saxifrage grows inland from the coast, in shaded side hills near creeks and streams, and is often found growing next to Mertens Saxifrage.

**What:** The flowers of California Saxifrage are clustered at the top of a single stem six to twelve inches tall. The oval-shaped leaves of this member of the Saxifrage family lie flat on the ground. The subtle markings and color of the flower head and stamens is intricately designed and worth a closer look.

# MARCH

**(53) Mertens Saxifrage**

**(54) Cream Cup**

**(55) Sun Cups**

**(56) California Saxifrage**

APRIL

Spring is here, and some obvious and compelling changes have occurred. Each day we have more light in the late afternoons and early evenings. In the air there is perfume of newly flowering plants and trees. The spicy smell of Pepperwood trees drifts through the canyon creeks and streams, mingling with the deep forest scent of the redwoods. A close look at the hills and woodlands tells you that the Buckeye trees have sprouted leaves overnight, and in the woods the Madrone trees are in full flower. The green hills and meadows are sown with masses of yellow Goldfields, and the newly plowed vineyards spill over with tides of cream-colored Meadow Foam. The coastal headlands are awakening from their winter sleep, while the high country still slumbers. In April, Nature's flower bloom is the beginning of a magnificent display of color, unfolding with the coming surge of spring, holding all things captive in the mystery of its remarkable beauty and grace.

## (57) Blue-eyed Grass *(Sisyrinchium bellum)*, A/S

**When:** The early blossoms of Blue-eyed Grass appear in late March or the beginning of April (March–May).

**Where:** Blue-eyed Grass is found throughout the county, blooming from the coast to the woodland hills and grassy meadows of the inland valleys. Some of the most extraordinary violet colors of Blue-eyed Grass are found on the coastal plateaus, whereas the colors may be more lavender to light blue in the inland meadows and fields. Orr Springs Road and Mountain House Road offer many fine displays of *S. bellum*.

**What:** A member of the Iris family, the flower petals of *S. bellum* vary in color from hues of pale blue to deep purple. The stems may reach a height of more than fifteen inches, with the flowers extended at the tip.

## (58) Wallflower *(Erysimum capitatum)*, A/S

**When:** Significant numbers of Wallflowers will bloom by mid-April (April–July).

**Where:** Wallflowers prefer rocky open slopes and canyon walls, most commonly east of Highway 101. Some of the finest examples of Wallflower shape and color are found on Route 162 west of Dos Rios, along the Eel River Canyon. Another excellent location for Wallflowers is Route 253 between Ukiah and Boonville.

**What:** Wallflowers are regal members of the Mustard family, and vary in color from brilliant orange to creamy yellow, contrasting beautifully against the canyon walls of our interior back roads. In late July, above 4,000 feet, the inner mountain version of *E. capitatum* reflects hues of the deepest orange, which are unusual and quite special within the wildflower color spectrum.

## (59) Redbud *(Cercis occidentalis)*, A/S

**When:** Redbud begins its attractive blooming cycle in late March, and reaches peak bloom by mid-April (April–May).

**Where:** In Mendocino County, Redbud thrives in the interior hills and foothill woodlands. Highway 20 from Ukiah east to the county line provides fine examples of Redbud. One of our favorite back roads for viewing it is Route 162 along the Eel River Canyon to Dos Rios and Covelo.

**What:** The beautiful magenta of Redbud flowers, set against the green of the countryside, is a delightful introduction to spring. Some early Native Americans split the slim branches of this member of the Pea family into threads to use in making their beautiful baskets.

## (60) Mule Ears *(Wyethia glabra)*, ½ A/S

**When:** You can expect to see a few Mule Ears blooming in late March, with the main bloom arriving around mid-April (March–June).

**Where:** *W. glabra* is found in wooded foothills, grassy hillsides, and along some of our back roads, like Mountain House Road and Eastside Road.

**What:** The generous yellow flowers of *W. glabra*, set off by the large green leaves, provide a colorful sight in the early spring. Mule Ears, so named because the leaves are said to resemble the ears of a mule, are members of the Aster family.

# APRIL

**(57) Blue-eyed Grass**

**(58) Wallflower**

**(59) Redbud**

**(60) Mule Ears**

## (61) Douglas's Violet – Golden Violet *(Viola douglasii)*, A/S +

**When:** You can expect to see Golden Violet blooming in early April (April–June).

**Where:** In the wet spring, Douglas's Violet blooms above 1,200 feet in the foothill woodlands and meadows of the inner valley mountains, and above 5,000 feet in the pine and fir forests of the high mountains during the dry summer months. Roads like Poonkinney, from Dos Rios to Covelo, and Route 162 to Mendocino Pass, provide excellent opportunities for viewing Douglas's Violet.

**What:** A member of the Violet family, Douglas's Violet reflects beautiful, golden amber colors in its large flower petals. Its feather-like leaves make this native plant easy to identify and enjoy.

## (62) Two-eyed Violet – Western Heart's-Ease *(Viola ocellata)*, A/S

**When:** Your first sightings of *V. ocellata* will be in early April (April–June).

**Where:** Look for Two-eyed Violet in woodland foothills and along shaded road banks of our inner valleys. Both Mill Creek Canyon east of Ukiah and Orr Springs Road, beyond the springs, are excellent places to look for *V. ocellata*. Several turns up Poonkinney Road east of Dos Rios will afford some restful searching for Western Heart's-Ease.

**What:** Two-eyed Violet is a small, delicate flower that belongs in the Violet family. The flower has two purple markings resembling eyes, and a yellow banding on the inner center of the petals. Heart's-Ease is a serene beauty with a quiet, shy look that, when hidden among other forest plants, will make you linger for a closer look.

## (63) Royal Larkspur *(Delphinium variegatum ssp. variegatum)*, A/S

**When:** You'll see the first Royal Larkspur blooming by early April (April–June).

**Where:** At least six species of *Delphinium* bloom in Mendocino county. *D. variegatum*, a less common species, is found on the woodland slopes and grassy meadows and fields of our interior valleys. Fine specimens of Royal Larkspur may be found in open, wooded grassy side hills along such roads as Mountain House Road and Low Gap Road.

**What:** *D. variegatum* is a member of the Buttercup family. The flowers are brilliant purple to violet, with an easily identifiable spur tip. The colors of Royal Larkspur will sometimes appear almost ink black against the gold browning of our hillside fields and meadows.

## (64) Woolly Sunflower *(Eriophyllum lanatum var. achillaeoides)*, ½ A/S

**When:** Woolly Sunflowers brighten the countryside in early April (April–July).

**Where:** Brush-covered side hills and rocky canyon slopes are where you'll find the Woolly Sunflower. Orr Springs Road, Low Gap Road, and Mountain View Road afford good viewing of *E. lanatum*.

**What:** Woolly sunflower is a member of the Aster family. The brilliant yellow ray flowers grow at the tips of loosely clumped stems, one to two feet tall, that are covered with silvery gray hairs. The radiant yellow of Woolly Sunflowers is striking when seen against the dry dirt banks and canyon walls along many of our back roads.

# APRIL

**(61) Douglas's Violet**

**(62) Two-eyed Violet**

**(63) Royal Larkspur**

**(64) Woolly Sunflower**

## (65) Manroot – Wild Cucumber (Marah oreganus), 2 × A/S

**When:** The large leaves and vine of Manroot will appear in March, the flowers in early April (March–June).

**Where:** Wild Cucumber may be found in brushy wooded foothills and open mixed hardwood and evergreen forests. You'll see *M. oreganus* growing along the sides of many of our back roads, such as Low Gap Road and Toll Road.

**What:** Manroot is a member of the Gourd family. *M. fabaceus* is another species of Manroot, more commonly found growing on the coastal bluffs; however, both species are very similar in flower size and shape. The female and male flowers grow on the same vine, but apart from one another.

## (66) Checker-Bloom (Sidalcea malvaeflora ssp. malvaeflora), ½ A/S

**When:** Checker Bloom, one of several species of *Sidalcea*, blooms in April (April–May).

**Where:** Several species of *Sidalcea* are common in our county. Checker Bloom is found from the coastal headlands to the open sunny meadows and wooded foothills of the inner valleys. The photograph on the opposite page was taken in a grassy field in Anderson Valley, alongside Route 128.

**What:** *S. malvaeflora* is a member of the Mallow Family.

## (67) Castilleja – Whisk Brooms (Castilleja densiflora), A/S

**When:** Whisk Brooms, a smaller version of Owl's Clover, blooms in early April (April–May).

**Where:** *C. densiflora*, though not common, and sometimes mistaken for Owl's Clover, grows on the open grassy hills and wooded foothills of our inner valleys. Such back roads as Poonkinney Road, between Dos Rios and Covelo, support large concentrations of Whisk Brooms; fewer specimens are found along Mountain House Road and Low Gap Road.

**What:** *C. densiflora* is a member of the Figwort family. Smaller and less striking in color than Owl's Clover, *C. densiflora* is nonetheless a charming addition to the grassy hills and meadows.

## (68) Chia (Salvia columbariae), A/S

**When:** Look for Chia to flower by the middle of April (April–May).

**Where:** Chia is not common in our county, but may be found on rocky hillside slopes and in the Mayacamas Mountains east of Ukiah. Chia grows in several places on or near the summit of the Boonville grade west of Ukiah. I have also observed it on rocky outcrops on Low Gap Road.

**What:** *S. columbariae* is a member of the Mint family. Chia deserves a closer look. Early Native Americans dried the seeds of the plant, which they then mixed with water and ate as gruel. It was said that a small portion of seeds could sustain a person through a long day's march. The stem may reach a height of two feet, with several rounded, spine-tipped heads, one above the other, having tiny whorls of blue flowers. While photographing Chia on the summit of the Boonville Road in 1992, I heard a voice say, "May God be with you." I thought my time had come. As I rose from my place on the rocky ground, I saw a tall man wearing a monk's robe and sandals. Witnessing for his God, he had walked from South America and was headed for Alaska. I mentioned the benefits of Chia for such a long journey. He thanked me for the information, and we soon parted as he continued on his chosen path. I never saw him again, and often wonder how he fared and whether he ever finished his mission.

# APRIL

**(65) Manroot**

**(66) Checker-Bloom**

**(67) Castilleja – Whisk Brooms**

**(68) Chia**

## (69) Cat's Ears – Pussy Ears *(Calochortus tolmiei)*, 1½ × A/S

**When:** We look forward with pleasure to finding the first Cat's Ears of the year. Depending on elevation, you can expect the early bloom during the first part of April (April–May).

**Where:** Pussy Ears are found throughout the county, at elevations of 800 feet and above, from the coast to the inner mountains, in open wooded foothills and brush, on dry road banks, and in moist open woods. My wife and I ride up Poonkinney Road, east of Dos Rios, where, on the first turn or two, we always find a wonderful display of Cat's Ears. Other roads with numerous Pussy Ears are Orr Springs Road and Fish Rock Road. The image on the opposite page was taken on Poonkinney Road.

**What:** *C. tolmiei* is a member of the Lily family. The petals, white or tinted slightly pink, are covered on the inside with fine hairs. Pussy Ears grow close to the ground in open clusters, and are always a delight to see and photograph.

## (70) Bird's Eye Gilia *(Gilia tricolor)*, A/S

**When:** The first Bird's Eye Gilia appear by early April, with the blooming cycle lasting well into May (April–June).

**Where:** You will find *G. tricolor* growing in open grassy meadows, hillsides, and wooded foothills. I notice Bird's Eye Gilia on back roads such as Orr Springs Road and Eastside Road. Large concentrations of *G. tricolor*, covering entire hillsides, are found farther to the east, in Lake and Colusa Counties.

**What:** Bird's Eye Gilia is a member of the Phlox family. You are blessed if you happen upon a hillside or road bank filled with the delicate lilac hue of these flowers.

## (71) Mountain Dogwood *(Cornus nuttallii)*, ¾ A/S

**When:** Look for the first Dogwood to bloom by mid-April (April–May).

**Where:** *C. nuttallii* is found in shaded moist woods near creeks and streams, and in our evergreen forests. We notice these beautiful trees on Highway 101 north of Willits in the spring and again in the late fall when the leaves turn color. Other areas for these native trees are the upper part of Reeves Canyon, Orr Springs Road, and the road leading to Ham Pass, north of Round Valley.

**What:** A member of the Dogwood family, *C. nuttallii* has large white bracts that appear as the petals. In the center are the heads of many small green flowers that resemble a large button. Perhaps Mountain Dogwood is most striking and conspicuous in late fall, when the leaves turn shell-pink to red. Several other species of Dogwood are found in the county; the most noticeable is Western Dogwood *(Cornus sericea ssp. occidentalis)*.

## (72) Diogenes' Lantern – Yellow Globe Lily *(Calochortus amabilis)*, A/S

**When:** You'll find the first Diogenes' Lanterns blooming by early April (April–May).

**Where:** Also called Yellow Globe Lily, or Golden Fairy Lantern, Diogenes' Lantern may be found throughout the county, in chaparral, on wooded foothills, and along many of our shaded grassy road banks. Robinson Creek Canyon and Mill Creek Canyon, both in the Ukiah Valley, are excellent places to look for Diogenes' Lantern.

**What:** A member of the Lily family, *C. amabilis* is the beautiful maiden of the spring wildflowers. The charming lemon-colored flowers are lovely, and should be observed without haste. While walking on Pine Ridge Road west of Ukiah, I counted more than 200 Yellow Globe Lilies in glorious bloom on a relatively small patch of grassy road bank.

**(70) Bird's Eye Gilia**

**(69) Cat's Ears**

**(71) Mountain Dogwood**

**(72) Diogenes' Lantern**

## (73) Camas – Camas Lily *(Camassia quamash)*, A / S

**When:** The first Camas Lilies may be seen blooming by mid-April (April–June).

**Where:** *C. quamash* is found growing at higher elevations, in wet fields and meadows of the inner valley mountains. A brilliant display of Camas at peak bloom occurs in early May several miles north of Willits in Little Lake Valley. Turn off Highway 101 at the north end of Little Lake Valley onto Reynolds Highway, and you'll be situated for the best viewing of the lovely Camas Lily.

**What:** Camas is a member of the Lily family. The great masses of *C. quamash* that bloom in Little Lake Valley are worth a special trip in May, as they fill the fields and meadows with their stunning deep-blue-to-violet color. Having traveled through our northern Sierra Nevada in the late spring and witnessed Camas in full bloom, I can honestly say that the Little Lake Valley display is the equal of those in the high-country meadows.

## (74) Scarlet Fritillary *(Fritillaria recurva)*, A / S

**When:** In early April at lower elevations, and in the middle of June at higher elevations, the lovely bloom of Scarlet Fritillary will greet you (April–June).

**Where:** *F. recurva* is not common in our county, but may be found east of Highway 101 in the inner coastal mountain range. Scarlet Fritillary grows on shaded wooded slopes and chaparral-covered hills above 1,500 feet. While driving from Dos Rios to Covelo on Poonkinney Road we counted more than twenty plants on a wooded bank above eye level. Other areas for Scarlet Fritillary include the logging road into Mt. Sanhedrin, under chaparral near the overlook into Round Valley, and the more than thirty plants blooming on a hillside meadow next to Route 162 above Mendocino Pass.

**What:** The enchanting bell-shaped flowers are deep orange-red, with yellow spotting both outside and inside the recurved petals. One beautiful specimen growing near Quincy, in the northern Sierra Nevada, had nine blossoms on a stem rising more than three feet tall. Scarlet Fritillary is a member of the Lily family.

## (75) Anderson Valley Mission Bells *(Fritillaria biflora var. biflora)*, 1½ × A / S

**When:** *F. biflora* blooms in early April and lasts into May (April–May).

**Where:** My wife and I have seen this rare plant blooming only in the Boonville Cemetery. One spring we counted more than seventy plants. These lovely flowers are on the endangered species list and deserve utmost care and protection.

**What:** I've taken the liberty of calling *F. biflora* "Anderson Valley Mission Bells." They are members of the Lily family, and their unique reddish-brown hue, with a small beige mark on the petal tips, makes them easily identified.

## (76) Chinese Houses *(Collinsia heterophylla)*, A / S

**When:** The first Chinese Houses will bloom by mid-April (April–June).

**Where:** *C. heterophylla* is found throughout the county, in grassy meadows, hillside slopes, and along many of our back roads. Beautiful displays of Chinese Houses bloom along Mountain House Road and Reeves Canyon Road. Mill Creek Canyon Road and the west-side trails of Mill Creek County Park will reward you with excellent sightings of *C. heterophylla*.

**What:** *C. heterophylla* resemble Chinese pagodas in shape, with whorls of beautifully marked petals on stems as tall as eighteen inches. Incredibly beautiful when seen individually or in mass, Chinese Houses are members of the Figwort family.

# APRIL

**(73) Camas**

**(74) Scarlet Fritillary**

**(75) Anderson Valley Mission Bells**

**(76) Chinese Houses**

## (77) Scarlet Columbine (Aquilegia formosa), A/S

**When:** The first Scarlet Columbine flowers bloom in early April. The blooming cycle for *A. formosa* lasts several months (April–June).

**Where:** Scarlet Columbine may be found from the immediate coast to the inner mountain range, in moist woods and road banks near canyon creeks and streams, and on brushy slopes. Highway 128 as it nears the coast, and Orr Springs Road, have fine displays of *A. formosa*.

**What:** A member of the Buttercup family, Scarlet Columbine has a unique airy quality and is a real beauty in design and color. The intricate blossoms are shaped like small red lanterns. Suspended from stems one to three feet tall, they add great charm and style to their surroundings.

## (78) Golden-eyed Grass (Sisyrinchium californicum), A/S

**When:** Golden-eyed Grass starts to bloom by mid-April (April–June).

**Where:** My wife and I look for Golden-eyed Grass on the coast. *S. californicum* grows in the wet coastal meadows and bogs found along Highway 1. Several bogs containing lovely concentrations of Golden-eyed Grass are found in the State Reserve headlands south of Fort Bragg, off Jefferson Way.

**What:** The bright yellow petals of Golden-eyed Grass are marked with distinctive dark veins that make this member of the Iris family a beautiful addition to the coastal fields and meadows. *S. californicum* reaches a height of more than two feet, and will form semi-dense colonies in the moist areas it inhabits.

## (79) Zigadene Lily – Star Lily – Death Camas (Zigadenus fremontii), A/S

**When:** You'll notice the first bloom of Star Lily by mid-April (April–June).

**Where:** *Z. fremontii* may be found near the coast on wooded brushy hillsides and slopes and along many of our back roads. Mountain View Road and Orr Springs Road are excellent places to see *Z. fremontii*.

**What:** Star Lily may grow to three feet in height, with numerous white-to-pale-yellow flowers bunched near the top of the stem. We have four or five species of *Zigadenus* in the county, all members of the Lily family. Another species found growing in the inland wooded foothills and grassy meadows is *Zigadenus micranthus*, or small-flowered Zigadene.

## (80) Yellow Stonecrop – Star-flowered Stonecrop (Sedum radiatum), A/S

**When:** The first Yellow Stonecrop will bloom around mid-April (April–June).

**Where:** *S. radiatum* seeks out the rocky hillsides and canyon walls of our wooded foothills. Beautiful examples of Yellow Stonecrop may be found on the Boonville—Ukiah Road and on Fish Rock Road. Others may be seen in upper Reeves Canyon and along the Eel River on Route 162.

**What:** Star-flowered Stonecrop is one of five or six species that grow in our county; all are members of the Stonecrop family. The leaves reflect a delicate shade of purple that is set off by the rich yellow of the star-shaped flowers. The color contrast between the flowers and the rocky terrain they inhabit is another extraordinary work of nature.

# APRIL

**(77) Scarlet Columbine**

**(78) Golden-eyed Grass**

**(79) Zigadene Lily**

**(80) Yellow Stonecrop**

## (81) Star Solomon Seal *(Smilacina stellata)*, 2 × A / S

**When:** The first flowers of *S. stellata* will show in late March or early April (March–June).

**Where:** Star Solomon Seal is found from the coast to the inner mountains, in damp mixed coastal forests, inner valley woodlands, and wet shaded foothills. I look for them in the Mill Creek Canyon in the Ukiah Valley, and along Highway 128 in the mixed evergreen forests of redwood, laurel, and tan oak near the Navarro River.

**What:** A member of the Lily family, Star Solomon Seal is one to two feet tall, with small clusters of star-like flowers and shiny green, lightly veined leaves. *S. stellata* is unobtrusive in the forest settings where it finds its home, quietly adding its small stature and graceful appearance to the other woodland plants.

## (82) Ceanothus – Buck Brush *(Ceanothus cuneatus var. cuneatus)*, ¾ A / S

**When:** Buck Brush starts its early bloom by mid-April (April–June).

**Where:** *C. cuneatus* inhabits open chaparral slopes and foothill woodlands throughout Mendocino County. In the late spring, on one of the many steep downturns of Highway 253 leading toward Ukiah, a remarkable sight greets you: an entire hillside covered with the pink-to-white blossoms of Buck Brush.

**What:** One of the many wild lilacs that bloom in Mendocino County, *C. cuneatus* is a member of the Buckthorn family.

## (83) Madrone Flowers – Madrono *(Arbutus menziesii)*, ½ A / S

**When:** The flowers of the beautiful Madrone tree bloom and hang in clusters toward the end of March and early April (March–May).

**Where:** The Madrone tree is distributed throughout Mendocino County's foothills and woodlands. Small forests of Madrono and their flowers may be seen on such back roads as Orr Springs Road, Low Gap Road, and Highway 253.

**What:** The Madrone tree is a member of the Heath family. Perhaps the finest specimens of *A. menziesii* are found in Mendocino and Humboldt Counties. The flowers are creamy white and urn-shaped, much like Manzanita flowers. The payoff comes from the fall months through December, when the berries form rich, orange-red clusters that festoon the trees like Christmas ornaments. The flowers and berries of the Madrone tree fill the hillside woodlands with color in the spring and again in the fall. Groves of Madrone, covered with berries in the fall, were called madrono by early Spanish Californians, because they resembled the strawberry trees, or madrono, native to Spain and other Mediterranean countries.

## (84) Clematis – Pipestems *(Clematis lasiantha)*, A / S +

**When:** Clematis reaches its peak bloom during the month of April (April–May).

**Where:** Pipestems are found throughout the county, in foothill mountains climbing over ceanothus, manzanita, and other shrubs. Excellent roads to view Clematis in bloom are Mountain View Road, Fish Rock Road, and the Old Toll Road.

**What:** *C. lasiantha* is a vine and a member of the Buttercup family. The creamy yellow flowers are sometimes difficult to see against the background of the shrubs they climb; be patient, because the flowers soon turn to seed pods, fluffy silver balls that are impossible to miss. Mark the spot for next year.

**(81) Star Solomon Seal**

**(82) Ceanothus**

**(83) Madrone Flowers**

**(84) Clematis**

## (85) Modesty *(Whipplea modesta)*, 2 × A/S

**When:** The first signs of the small, attractive *W. modesta* plant and its flowers appear in early April (April–June).

**Where:** Modesty may be found growing from the coastal woods to the moist foothill woodlands of the inner valleys. Shaded, wooded side roads in areas such as Jackson State Forest or Orr Springs Road are likely places to find it.

**What:** *W. modesta* is a member of the Mock Orange family, and is recognizable as a creeping plant with trailing stems that are rooted. The tiny flowers form a small rounded head on erect stems three to four inches tall. A walk along most paths in the wooded foothills and moist redwoods will introduce you to this lovely little plant. I always find several on the upper trail of Low Gap County Park, in Ukiah.

## (86) Redwood Violet *(Viola sempervirens)*, 2 × A/S

**When:** Redwood Violets flower by the middle of March, and reach their peak bloom by April, lasting well into June (March–June).

**Where:** As their name implies, look for these violets on the floor of our redwood forests. Clusters of *V. sempervirens* are found in the mossy groundcover and floor of second-growth redwoods and mixed forests in areas along many of our coastal back roads. Orr Springs Road, Cameron Road, and Gualala River Road all have fine displays of *V. sempervirens*.

**What:** A member of the Violet family, Redwood Violets form lovely carpets of pale yellow in the brown forest duff, a welcome sight in the darkened woods.

## (87) Orange Bush Monkey Flower *(Mimulus aurantiacus)*, A/S

**When:** Orange Bush Monkey Flower starts its early bloom by mid-April and continues to bloom well into July (April–July).

**Where:** *M. aurantiacus* is found blooming throughout the entire county, from the coast to the inner mountains. Orange Bush Monkey Flower makes a fine showing on the open rocky hillsides and cliffs of many of our back roads.

**What:** A member of the Figwort family, Orange Bush Monkey Flower is a woody shrub. On Orr Springs Road and Highway 20 near Lake Mendocino, you'll find open side hills covered with *M. aurantiacus*, creating a sea of color that is striking in its intensity.

## (88) Penstemon – Hillside Penstemon *(Penstemon heterophyllus)*, 2 × A/S

**When:** Look for Penstemon to bloom by mid-April (April–June).

**Where:** *P. heterophyllus* likes the dry, open road banks, dirt side hills, and the wooded foothills of our inner valleys and mountains. The violet-blue color of Penstemon may be seen on the Boonville–Ukiah Road and Orr Springs Road. The first part of Lake Mendocino Drive on the north side of Lake Mendocino always has a nice show of Penstemon.

**What:** During a spring rain, the violet-blue color of *P. heterophyllus* is iridescent. The eye is drawn immediately to the small bouquet of flowers and the beautiful colors of this member of the Figwort family. Hillside Penstemon does well in cultivation and is popular at native-plant sales. At least ten species of Penstemon grow in Mendocino County.

**(85) Modesty**

**(86) Redwood Violet**

**(87) Orange Bush Monkey Flower**

**(88) Penstemon**

## (89) Yarrow *(Achillea millefolium)*, A/S

**When:** Yarrow may be seen blooming as early as March, with the flowering cycle lasting well into July (March–July).

**Where:** Yarrow grows throughout the county, from the coastal headlands to the grassy meadows and wooded foothills of the inner mountains. A walk through the woods and grassy slopes of Low Gap County Park or the headlands of Manchester Beach State Park will introduce you to Yarrow.

**What:** *A. millefolium* is a member of the Aster family. Yarrow has a long history of virtues; one of the more popular uses was to steep the leaves in hot water and apply them to cuts and bruises to speed the healing process. Yarrow leaves are narrow, dissected, and quite feathery in appearance.

## (90) Star Flower *(Trientalis latifolia)*, A/S +

**When:** You'll see the first delicate star flowers blooming by mid-April if not sooner (April–June).

**Where:** *T. latifolia* may be found in foothill woodlands and openings in shaded forests, from the coast to the inner mountains. I enjoy looking for Star Flowers when I walk in places like Low Gap County Park and Mill Creek Canyon.

**What:** A member of the Primrose family, Trientalis has one or more small delicate flowers resting atop several slender three-to-four-inch stems. Before the threadlike stems and flowers appear, you'll see a cluster of oval-shaped leaves at the top of a leafless main stem, making you wonder what manner of plant it might be and whether it will flower. The small star-shaped flowers may be white or pink.

## (91) Bleeding Heart *(Dicentra formosa)*, 2 × A/S

**When:** *D. formosa* begins to flower in early April (April–July).

**Where:** Bleeding Heart does best in moist shaded woodlands near creeks and streams, from the coast to the high mountain meadows and forest openings of the inner mountain range. Russian Gulch State Park on the coast, and the wet meadows of the high inner mountains near Mendocino Pass, provide excellent environments for Bleeding Heart to thrive.

**What:** *D. formosa* is a member of the Poppy family. The flowers range in color from pink to red-purple and occasionally white. The feathery, lace-like leaves will show before the flat heart-shaped flowers appear. While hiking near the Mendocino Pass in late June several years ago, I happened upon a beautiful colony of Bleeding Heart that covered and spilled over a large rocky outcrop, giving the effect of an enchanting waterfall of purple flowers.

## (92) Fairy Bells *(Disporum hookeri)*, 1½ × A/S

**When:** A small, modest flower, Fairy Bells may be found blooming in late March or early April (April–May).

**Where:** *D. hookeri* grows inland in moist shaded forests near creeks and streams. The redwoods along Highway 128, and the Mill Creek Canyon and Orr Springs areas, offer fine displays of Fairy Bells.

**What:** The Fairy Bell is a member of the Lily family. The veined leaves hide the tiny greenish-white flowers so effectively that unless you bend or crawl to peer underneath, you may never see these hidden flowers of the forest.

# APRIL

**(89) Yarrow**

**(90) Star Flower**

**(91) Bleeding Heart**

**(92) Fairy Bells**

## (93) Dutchman's Pipe – Pipevine *(Aristolochia californica)*, A/S

**When:** Dutchman's Pipe has not yet been found growing wild in Mendocino County, but there's a good chance it will be. The flowers begin blooming in March or early April (March–May).

**Where:** If found by some lucky wildflower enthusiast, Pipevine will be climbing over fences and thickets in brushy open country east of Highway 101. Perhaps Dutchman's Pipe may be found east of Willits in areas such as Hearst or the brushy foothills of Round Valley. The photograph on the opposite page was taken in the backyard of the Dwights' home in Redwood Valley. The plant in their yard came from a specimen growing wild in the foothills of the Sacramento Valley.

**What:** Pipevine is a member of the Birthwort family, and is used as a decorative plant for landscaping. The woody stems of this climbing vine support greenish, odd-shaped flowers with brown markings. The flowers bloom before the attractive heart-shaped leaves appear. I find Dutchman's Pipe interesting and exotic; hopefully someone will soon find it growing wild in our county.

## (94) Scarlet Pimpernel *(Anagallis arvensis)*, 2 × A/S

**When:** The attractive salmon-colored flowers of Scarlet Pimpernel start blooming in April (April–June).

**Where:** *A. arvensis* is common from the coast to the inland valleys, and is found in open grassy fields and meadows, and on brushy side-hill slopes. On the coast, Scarlet Pimpernel is almost always found on open ground, in areas such as Manchester Beach State Park or the headlands north of Fort Bragg. I look for clumps of the small, salmon-pink (and sometimes blue) blossoms in open fields and meadows in such areas as the Hopland Field Station and along the grassy side hills of Low Gap Road.

**What:** A native of the Old World, Scarlet Pimpernel is a member of the Primrose family.

## (95) Forget-me-not *(Myosotis latifolia)*, 1½ × A/S

**When:** It wouldn't seem like spring without Forget-me-not flowers. Look for *M. latifolia* to bloom from March through June (March–June).

**Where:** Some of the most beautiful flowers of *M. latifolia* are found in moist redwood forests near seeps and streams. We have encountered masses of Forget-me-nots carpeting the forest floor east of Rockport on Highway 1, creating a sea of bright blue in the forest dusk.

**What:** Common Forget-me-not is a member of the Borage family and is native to northwest Africa.

## (96) Tomcat Clover *(Trifolium willdenovii)*, 2 × A/S

**When:** Tomcat Clover blooms from early April to July (April–July).

**Where:** *T. willdenovii* grows profusely on grassy slopes, meadows, and fields inland from the coast. I find dense patches of *T. willdenovii* on the banks of such roads as Mountain House Road, Orr Springs Road, and Route 162 east of Covelo.

**What:** Tomcat Clover is a member of the Pea family and is one of many species of Clover found in the county. When in full bloom, the round, reddish-pink heads are very colorful in the golden grass of late spring and early summer.

**(93) Dutchman's Pipe**

**(94) Scarlet Pimpernel**

**(95) Forget-me-not**

**(96) Tomcat Clover**

## (97) Linanthus *(Linanthus parviflorus)*, A /S +

**When:** The colorful white-to-pink blossoms of Linanthus appear in early April, with the blooming cycle lasting into June (April–June).

**Where:** *L. parviflorus* is found in grassy open foothills, on rocky canyon walls, and in shaded woodlands. I find the beautiful Linanthus flowers growing along the dirt and grassy banks of back roads like Mountain House Road, Low Gap Road, and Route 162 from Longvale to Dos Rios.

**What:** Linanthus is a member of the Phlox family. The color varies from rose pink to white. The small bouquets of Linanthus growing along our county back roads will attract your attention and entice you to a closer look. The photograph of Linanthus on the opposite page was taken on Mountain House Road.

## (98) Purple Owl's Clover *(Castillega exserta ssp. exserta)*, A/S

**When:** You can expect to see the lovely color of Purple Owl's clover blooming by the second week in April (April–May).

**Where:** Although not common in Mendocino County, Purple Owl's Clover is found scattered along the coast, inland in open fields and meadows, and along such back roads as Route 128 south of Boonville. The coastal version of *C. exserta* grows in abundance on the stable dunes of Manchester Beach State Park. In a good year, one of the finer displays of Owl's Clover may be found in a small field on the Pinole Rancheria adjacent to Orr Springs Road (this is private property and is not to be disturbed).

**What:** A member of the Figwort family, Owl's Clover is spotty in Mendocino County. To see *C. exserta* at its best you need to be in the high meadows of the Sierra Nevada or in our neighboring counties to the east. When found in large colonies, the massed hue of Owl's Clover is an extraordinary sight, turning meadows and hills into bright magentas that shimmer and vibrate in the clear mountain air.

## (99) Hillside Pea *(Lathyrus vestitus)*, A/S

**When:** Hillside Pea will flower and show color by early April (April–June).

**Where:** You'll find Hillside Pea growing in wooded foothills and brushy meadows from the coast to the inner valleys. Lathyrus is a vine that loves to climb on old fence lines, small trees, and bushy shrubs. I look for it along the lower trail in Low Gap County Park, and on many of our back roads, like Orr Springs Road and Low Gap Road.

**What:** *L. vestitus* is a member of the Pea family. The flowers of Hillside Pea combine a number of different colors such as orange-brown, and lavender-blue. These colors are subtle and very attractive, adding much enjoyment to any hike through the woods and fields.

## (100) Sour Clover – Bull clover *(Trifolium fucatum)*, A/S

**When:** Sour Clover's colorful shades of yellow and pink should be noticeable by early April (April–June).

**Where:** *T. fucatum* is found from the coast inland, in open fields and meadows, and along the grassy road banks of many of our back roads. Large masses of Bull Clover are found on Mountain House Road, and on Route 253 between Ukiah and Boonville.

**What:** Sour Clover is a member of the Pea family. I always stop for a closer look at Bull Clover when it reaches peak bloom. The pale yellow-to-pink hue of the blossoms is enhanced when the flowers inflate into large sacs, filling roadside banks and ditches with lovely color.

# APRIL

**(97) Linanthus**

**(98) Purple Owl's Clover**

**(99) Hillside Pea**

**(100) Sour Clover**

## (101) Butter and Eggs – Johnny Tuck (Triphysaria eriantha), A/S +

**When:** Butter and Eggs appears in late March, with the blooming cycle lasting well into May (April–June).

**Where:** Butter and Eggs, also called Johnny Tuck, is commonly seen in the grassy fields and hillsides of our inland valleys. I find Johnny Tuck in abundance In Low Gap County Park and along such back roads as Mountain House Road and Eastside Road. Potter Valley and Round Valley also support large concentrations of Johnny Tuck.

**What:** *T. eriantha* is a member of the Figwort family. The small, sac-like flowers grow on stems six to ten inches tall. When seen from a distance, Johnny Tuck reflects unique shades of pale yellow, making the flowers easy to identify.

## (102) Red Maids (Calandrinia ciliata), A/S

**When:** Red Maids first appear in late March and last well into May (April–June).

**Where:** Red Maids are found from the coastal headlands and dunes to the inner valleys, grassy meadows, and fields. Coastal areas such as Manchester Beach State Park, and back roads such as Route 128 southeast of Boonville, and Mountain House Road between Route 128 and Hopland, offer quiet spots where you can seek and find Red Maids.

**What:** Well established in our county, *C. ciliata* is a member of the Purslane family. A native plant, Red Maids' habitat extends to northwest South America. Red Maids are low-growing plants with bright-red flower petals; their rich color will surely catch your eye and make you stop for a closer look.

## (103) Woodland Star (Lithophragma affine), A/S

**When:** Woodland Star makes its first appearance by early April (April–June).

**Where:** I look for *L. affine* on wooded side hills, on the shaded road banks of our inland valleys, and along our mountain back roads. My wife and I enjoy looking for Woodland Stars on such roads as the Old Toll Road and Route 175 east of Hopland. Other areas for viewing Woodland Star include Low Gap County Park and Route 162 east of Covelo.

**What:** The pure-white flowers of the Woodland Star are deeply notched, with as many as six to ten flowers growing on a single stem that may reach a height of eighteen inches. Woodland Star is a member of the Saxifrage family.

## (104) Fiddle Neck (Amsinckia intermedia), A/S +

**When:** The very first Fiddle Necks will bloom in late March or early April (March–June).

**Where:** Fiddle Neck grows in open fields and slopes, from the coast to the inner mountains. My wife and I have found great masses blooming in the grassy fields east of Hopland on the Old Toll Road.

**What:** *A. intermedia* is a member of the Borage family. The flowers are shaped like fiddles. When massed in a field, they produce a burnt-orange hue that is unusual and quite attractive.

# APRIL

**(101) Butter and Eggs**

**(102) Red Maids**

**(103) Woodland Star**

**(104) Fiddle Neck**

## (105) Farewell to Spring (Clarkia amoena ssp. amoena), A/S

**When:** The beautiful Farewell to Spring makes its first appearance by mid-April, and much to our delight, remains with us into early summer (April–July).

**Where:** *C. amoena* may be found throughout the county, from the coast to the inner mountain range. It prefers grassy meadows and fields, and many of the road banks on our back roads. During the month of May, Eastside Road between Ukiah and Hopland, and Low Gap Road west of Ukiah, provide excellent viewing of Clarkia in glorious full bloom.

**What:** Farewell to Spring is a member of the Evening Primrose family. It is variable in color, ranging from pink to magenta and lavender. The petals may be marked with wine-colored blotches or not marked at all. Clarkia grows in large clusters as tall as three feet, with numerous flowers on one stem. The superb color and overall effect of Farewell to Spring will lift your heart and bring a smile to your face.

## (106) Red Onion – Sickle-Leaved Onion (Allium falcifolium), A/S

**When:** Sickle-Leaved Onion begins to bloom in mid-April (April–June).

**Where:** *A. falcifolium* blooms mainly east of Highway 101, in serpentine, rocky gravel flats in the higher elevations of the inner mountain range. By mid-June, a fine display of Red Onion is located on the gravelly windswept summit of Anthony Peak. Other areas include the rocky, brush-covered slopes above the Hopland Field Station.

**What:** Sickle-Leaved Onion, a member of the Lily family, has a beautiful head of urn-shaped flowers supported by a ribbon-like stem with flat, broad leaves. The umbel of rose-colored flowers appears to spring from the rocky soil, a most interesting sight on the barren slopes of Anthony Peak.

## (107) Ceanothus – Blue Blossom (Ceanothus thyrsiflorus), A/S

**When:** One of the many species of wild lilac found in Mendocino County, *C. thyrsiflorus* blooms from early May to late July (May–July).

**Where:** Blue Blossom is found from the coast inland to Highway 101. Magnificent specimens of Blue Blossom the size of small trees are found on the Greenwood–Elk Road between Elk and Hendy State Park, and on Orr Springs Road east of Comptche.

**What:** *C. thyrsiflorus* is a member of the Buckthorn family.

## (108) Hottentot Fig – Marigold Fig (Carpobrotus edulis), A/S

**When:** Hottentot Fig blooms throughout the year; the flowers are at their peak during the spring and summer months (March–Sept.).

**Where:** Marigold Fig is found on the coastal road banks and dunes, primarily north of Fort Bragg from MacKerricher State Park to Ten Mile River.

**What:** *C. edulis* is one of several plants that were brought in to stabilize dunes and coastal road banks along the immediate coast. Widely planted for that reason, *C. edulis* has over the years become naturalized. Hottentot Fig, a South African transplant, is a member of the Carpet Weed family. It ranges from southern Oregon to Mexico.

**(105) Farewell to Spring**

**(106) Red Onion**

**(107) Ceanothus**

**(108) Hottentot Fig**

## (109) Beach Evening Primrose *(Camissonia cheiranthifolia)*, A/S +

**When:** Beach Primrose has a long blooming cycle, starting in early May and continuing into late August (May–Aug.).

**Where:** Beach Primrose is found on the coastal dunes and strands along Mendocino County's coastline. Many areas of the coastline where sand dunes are prevalent, as in Manchester Beach State Park and the stable dunes of MacKerricher State Park, provide excellent viewing of *C. cheiranthifolia*.

**What:** A member of the Evening Primrose family, *C. cheiranthifolia* is a prostrate plant with gray-green oval leaves. Beach Primrose is an attractive little plant that adds color and texture to the areas where it is found. The small yellow flowers are nestled among the leaves, presenting lovely bouquets that spread and scatter among the coastal sand hills. *C. cheiranthifolia* ranges from the Channel Islands to the southwest part of the Oregon coast.

## (110) Dune Collinsia – Dune Chinese Houses *(Collinsia corymbosa)*, A/S +

**When:** The early bloom of Dune Collinsia, or Dune Chinese Houses, becomes noticeable during the first part of April (April–May).

**Where:** In Mendocino County, *C. corymbosa* is found only along the coastal dunes and sand hills between Fort Bragg and Ten Mile River. The stable dunes and sand hills in this area support fine specimens of Dune Collinsia.

**What:** A member of the Figwort family, the small, robust Dune Collinsia is a scarce California endemic, and is considered rare and endangered by the California Native Plant Society. The low, trailing, branched stems with green oval leaves support a rounded head of small, whorled pink-and-white flowers. *C. corymbosa* is particularly attractive when mixed among other coastal plants such as Yellow Sand Verbena and Beach Artemisia (known as Beach Sagewort). The photograph of *C. corymbosa* on the opposite page was taken on the sand hills north of Fort Bragg. Dune Collinsia is a fragile, lovely plant that should be left alone.

## (111) Menzies' Wallflower *(Erysimum menziesii ssp. menziesii)*, ¾ A/S

**When:** *E. menziesii* begins its blooming cycle toward the end of March or in early April (March–April).

**Where:** Menzies' Wallflower is found directly on the coast, primarily north of Fort Bragg in the sand hills and stable dunes near MacKerricher State Park.

**What:** A rare plant, *E. menziesii* is a member of the Mustard family. The bright-yellow flowers are formed into shapes like small pagodas, sometimes in clumps or on single stems, with the dark-green spatula-shaped leaves placed at the base. *E. menziesii* has been placed on the federal list of endangered species and, if found, should be left alone.

## (112) Coastal Buttercups *(Ranunculus flammula)*, A/S +

**When:** Coastal Buttercups bloom from late March through July (March–July).

**Where:** Ranunculus is found on many of our coastal headlands, perhaps most noticeably on the bluffs north of Pudding Creek and near Manchester Beach State Park.

**What:** A beautiful, low-growing plant of extraordinary color, *R. flammula* is a member of the Buttercup family.

**(109) Beach Evening Primrose**

**(110) Dune Collinsia**

**(111) Menzies' Wallflower**

**(112) Coastal Buttercups**

## (113) Dune Phacelia (Phacelia insularis var. continentis), A/S +

**When:** The early bloom of Dune Phacelia appears during the first week in March. The flowering cycle lasts through the end of April (March–April).

**Where:** *P. insularis* inhabits a very narrow environmental zone restricted to sandhills, dunes, and ocean bluffs around the Fort Bragg area. MacKerricher State Park and north toward Ten Mile are likely places to look for Dune Phacelia.

**What:** *Phacelia insularis* is member of the Waterleaf family. The California Native Plant Society has placed it on the rare and endangered species list. The tiny purplish flowers form small mats that lie prostrate in the sand and on moist grassy headlands. Because of the small size of the flowers, these plants are difficult to spot. If found, they should be left alone.

## (114) Fort Bragg Manzanita (Arctostaphylos nummularia), A/S +

**When:** Fort Bragg Manzanita blooms from March through June (March–June).

**Where:** You'll find *A. nummularia* ranging from Gualala north to Fort Bragg. This species of Manzanita is found on the east side of Highway 1, where it inhabits brushy areas along such back roads as Iverson Road near Gualala, and Caspar–Little Lake Road east of Mendocino Village. Large concentrations of Fort Bragg Manzanita inhabit the pygmy forest between Orr Springs Road and Little River.

**What:** *A. nummularia* is a low-growing shrub, variable in size up to two feet in height. In most cases the branches are prostrate, the typically small rounded leaves sometimes having sharp tips. When it is in full bloom, small white-to-pink urn-shaped flowers cover the plant. *A. nummularia* is a member of the Heath family.

## (115) Oso Berry (Oemleria cerasiformis), A/S

**When:** Look for the early bloom of Oso Berry in late March or early April (March–April).

**Where:** Oso Berry is found from the coast to the inner mountains, in mixed evergreen forests and in chaparral east of Mill Creek Road, in the Mayacamas mountain range. The photograph on the opposite page was taken on the county road leading to Lake Pillsbury.

**What:** A member of the Rose family, *O. cerasiformis* in bloom is a lovely, scented shrub that's usually found as a single plant. Occasionally, you'll find thickets of Oso Berry that will add much to your enjoyment of a wildflower trip. Oso Berry grows from three to five feet tall.

## (116) Dog Violet (Viola adunca), 2 × A/S

**When:** At least fifteen species of *Viola* inhabit Mendocino County. The bloom cycle runs from March through July.

**Where:** *V. adunca* is widespread throughout the county, and may be found from ocean bluffs to the high mountains of the inner coastal range. The photograph of the Dog Violet on the opposite page was taken in April on the headlands off Jefferson Lane, south of Fort Bragg.

**What:** Violets belong in their own private family. The Viola family has produced both wild and cultivated Violets, admired throughout the world for their beauty.

# APRIL

**(113) Dune Phacelia**

**(114) Fort Bragg Manzanita**

**(115) Oso Berry**

**(116) Dog Violet**

MAY

The month of May in Mendocino County is the time to witness the great display of wildflowers that Nature orchestrates. The expanse between the middle of April and the end of May provides an amazing, unparalleled show of different wildflower species. The coastal flowers are beginning to bloom on the seaside cliffs and meadows, while the inner valleys and foothills are ablaze with color. The snowmelt in the high mountains has the look of early spring, with the flowers soon to follow. Many species of wildflowers that bloomed in March are still with us, along with the flowers of April, and to these we can add the spectacular bloom of May. But look closely, because summer is lurking, and the sudden warmth of May always comes as a surprise. The hillsides and inland valleys that have been green since March will give way to a burnt gold color that I have learned to love, and in an instant the spring flower display has ended, setting the stage for the next act. But let's not hurry; as we continue our journey, we can pause for a while on a hillside trail or in a coastal meadow. Perhaps in our quiet we will feel the wind on our faces and the gentle hand of Nature leading us into peaceful harmony.

## (117) Glacier Lily *(Erythronium grandiflorum var. pallidum)*, A/S

**When:** Because the Glacier Lily is found only at high elevations, the time of bloom may vary due to snow conditions. The most likely bloom period is during the last part of May or early June (May–June).

**Where:** My wife and I found several patches of *E. grandiflorum* blooming near the summit of Anthony Peak during the first week in June 2002. Due to the late snowstorms that year, the normal blooming cycles of many flowers of the inner mountain range were delayed by several weeks. To my knowledge, Anthony Peak might be the only area in Mendocino County where *E. grandiflorum* is found. Glacier Lilies range from the Cascades to the Rocky Mountains, but are rare in the Sierra Nevada.

**What:** Yellow-flowered *E. grandiflorum* is a member of the Lily family.

## (118) Wild Mock Orange *(Philadelphus lewisii)*, A/S

**When:** The species *P. lewisii* is found above 3,000 feet, and blooms from early May to mid-June (May–July).

**Where:** Wild Mock Orange may be found in foothill canyons and on wooded grassy slopes near creeks and streams. I photographed the flowers on the opposite page on Route 162, east of Covelo, in a seep spring at the 3,000-foot level. In this same area, we found numerous Philadelphus shrubs lining a small canyon creek. They were in full bloom, making a lovely display of color against the browning countryside.

**What:** *P. lewisii* is a member of the Mock Orange family. A large shrub with well-placed branches, it puts on a marvelous exhibition of pure-white flowers when in full bloom. Native to our county, Mock Orange does well in cultivation, and makes a fine addition to any home garden.

## (119) Bitter Cherry *(Prunus emarginata)*, A/S

**When:** Depending on elevation, Bitter Cherry's blooming cycle lasts from April to late June (May–June).

**Where:** *P. emarginata* is found in the higher elevations east of Highway 101. We find large thickets of Bitter Cherry near the summit of Anthony Peak and along back roads leading to Hull Mountain and Sanhedrin. The image on the opposite page was taken below the lookout on Anthony Peak, at an elevation above 7,000 feet.

**What:** A member of the Rose family, the medium-sized Bitter Cherry shrub is a glorious sight when its abundant white flowers are in full bloom. An additional visual treat awaits you when the bright red berries form in the fall.

## (120) Utah Service Berry *(Amelanchier utahensis)*, 1½ × A/S

**When:** The blooming cycle of *A. utahensis* depends on elevation: near sea level it blooms toward the end of March; and at elevations above 5,000 feet, from May–June.

**Where:** Utah Service Berry is found throughout Mendocino County in areas such as MacKerricher State Park, Low Gap County Park, and the higher elevations of the inner mountain range on the roads to Mendocino Pass and Anthony Peak.

**What:** A member of the Rose family, Utah Service Berry is a large, handsome shrub.

# MAY

**(117) Glacier Lily**

**(118) Wild Mock Orange**

**(119) Bitter Cherry**

**(120) Utah Service Berry**

## (121) Milkwort (Polygala californica), A/S +

**When:** You'll see the small flowers of Milkwort blooming by early May (May–July).

**Where:** Milkwort is common to many different habitats, and is found from the coast to the wooded foothills and shaded chaparral of our interior valleys. The wooded foothills of Low Gap Road and Orr Springs Road are the areas where I seek and find the small Milkwort flowers.

**What:** *Polygala californica* is a member of the Milkwort family. The small pea-shaped flowers and oblong leaves grow on woody stems up to six inches long. When you bend down for your first close look at *P. californica*, you'll find, much to your delight, that the plant and flowers resemble miniature shrubs.

## (122) Purple Nightshade (Solanum parishii), A/S +

**When:** Depending on its habitat, you might see Purple Nightshade blooming in early March or in late July. I've put *S. parishii* in late May as the most likely flowering month (March–July).

**Where:** A similar-looking nightshade, *Solanum xanti*, is found in dry wooded foothills and chaparral-covered slopes, mainly east of Highway 101. Roads that will give you a peek at this attractive, small bushy plant are the Toll Road east of Hopland, and Mill Creek Canyon in the Mayacamas Mountains. For more adventurous souls, the road to Ham Pass off Route 162 will provide more stunning displays of the high-mountain nightshade *Solanum parishii*.

**What:** *Solanum parishii* and *Solanum xanti* are small shrub-like plants in the Nightshade family. Very similar in appearance, the clusters of violet-to-blue-colored flowers of Purple Nightshade appear brilliant against the stark dry foothills of early summer. While driving along such roads as the Toll Road, or walking in the upper part of Mill Creek Canyon, it's impossible to pass the attractive nightshade flowers without stopping for a closer look.

## (123) Forktooth Ookow – Brodiaea (Dichelostemma congestum), A/S +

**When:** The violet-to-blue flowers of the Forktooth Ookow bloom by the second week in May (May–July).

**Where:** *D. congestum*, called ookow by early Native Americans, is found on the dry grassy hills and wooded slopes of our inner valley foothills. Many of the county's back roads, like Orr Springs Road, Low Gap Road, and Route 162 to Round Valley, provide excellent opportunities for viewing this late-blooming species of *Dichelostemma*.

**What:** A member of the Lily family, Brodiaea grows on a stout stem reaching a height of more than three feet. Many small violet-to-blue flowers are congested at the head of the stem in the form of an umbel. What a lovely sight the colorful ookow makes in our fields and meadows as it bends and sways in the slightest summer breeze.

## (124) Fringed Pink (Silene hookeri), A/S

**When:** The lovely flowers of Fringed Pink bloom in early May (May–June).

**Where:** *S. hookeri* grows primarily on shaded grassy banks in the woodland meadows and hills northeast of Willits. A quiet area to look for Fringed Pink is on the grassy banks of Walker Road just south of Willits; other areas for looking pleasure are Poonkinney Road off Route 162, and the foothills near Round Valley.

**What:** A member of the Pink family, *S. hookeri* is beautiful both in shape and color. The delicate pink petals appear cut as though Nature's own gardener had used pinking shears.

# MAY

**(121) Milkwort**

**(122) Purple Nightshade**

**(123) Forktooth Ookow**

**(124) Fringed Pink**

## (125) Yellow Pond Lily (Nuphar luteum), ½ A/S

**When:** Yellow Pond Lilies begin blooming by late April (April–June).

**Where:** *N. luteum* may be found growing in coastal lagoons, on the edges of quiet rivers and streams and inland on small ponds and lakes. The photograph on the opposite page was taken in a small lake just west of Laytonville. Stripped to my underwear, I was standing in two feet of water, my camera set on a tripod, when I noticed a group of people showing concern—but from a safe distance. I explained what I was doing to no avail; they assumed I had lost my mind, that I was one of "those city folk." I took my shot and made good my escape.

**What:** *N. luteum* is a member of the Water Lily family. The large green leaves can partially cover a small lake. For me, it's always exciting to discover some hidden pond in a forest setting and find the water filled with the bright-yellow blossoms of the Pond Lily.

## (126) Bear Grass – Basket Grass (Xerophyllum tenax), ½ A/S

**When:** The exotic flowers of Bear Grass start blooming in Late May (May–July).

**Where:** Bear Grass is almost always found growing near the coast in openings among stunted trees, huckleberry, and rhododendron. Look for Bear Grass several miles inland from the coast, on roads such as Cameron Road and Little Lake Road.

**What:** *X. tenax* is a member of the Lily family. The clusters of small white flowers form a rounded spike at the end of a thick stem from one to five feet tall. Some early Native Americans used the wiry grass-like leaves in weaving their beautiful baskets. The clumps of leaves appear first, and it may be several years before the flowers appear, giving forth their seed at maturity and then dying, thus making room for the next generation.

## (127) Spotted Coral-root (Corallorhiza maculata), 2 × A/S

**When:** You should find Spotted Coral-root blooming by mid-May (May–June).

**Where:** *C. maculata* is found growing throughout the county in mixed conifer forests and woodlands from the coast to the inner mountain range. I find Coral-root growing near the coast on Mountain View Road and Orr Springs Road. Other areas where Coral-root does well include the forests leading to Black Butte near Mendocino Pass and Mt. Sanhedrin west of Lake Pillsbury.

**What:** Spotted Coral-root is a member of the Orchid family. The plants normally grow in small colonies, the brownish-red stems reaching a height of twenty inches. The small, orchid-shaped flowers cluster near the top of the stem, and are almost always white with reddish-purple spots.

## (128) Wood Rose (Rosa gymnocarpa), A/S +

**When:** The small Wood Rose begins to flower during the early part of May (May–June).

**Where:** *R. gymnocarpa* is scattered about the county in wooded foothills and shady forests from the coast to the inner mountains.

**What:** The eight or nine species of wild rose growing in the county are members of the Rose family. The Wood Rose is somewhat shy and won't be found in large groups; the flowers choose to be solitary. Their lovely shade of pink will draw your attention immediately. The photograph of the Wood Rose on the opposite page was taken on a wooded side hill on Low Gap Road.

# MAY

**(125) Yellow Pond Lily**

**(126) Bear Grass**

**(127) Spotted Coral-root**

**(128) Wood Rose**

## (129) Blue-headed Gilia – Globe Gilia *(Gilia capitata ssp. capitata)*, A/S +

**When:** Look for Globe Gilias to bloom by mid-April or early May (May–June).

**Where:** *G. capitata* is found on open sunny banks and in wooded foothills from the ocean to the inner mountains. I look for Blue-headed Gilia on the grassy banks of such back roads as Mountain House Road, Orr Springs Road, and Route 162 east of Covelo.

**What:** Blue-headed Gilia is a member of the Phlox family. The smoky blue color of the ball-shaped flower head is made up of many small blossoms that sit on erect stems up to three feet tall. *G. capitata* is at its best when found growing in large clusters on grassy side hills or road banks on a sunny spring day.

## (130) Mariposa Lily *(Calochortus vestae)*, ½ A/S

**When:** I start looking for the first bloom of *C. vestae* in early May. It always gives me great pleasure and comfort to find the very first Mariposa Lilies. For a peek at the first flowers of the year, I search the grassy hillsides next to Low Gap Road; so far, I've never been disappointed (May–June).

**Where:** *C. vestae* is found blooming on the sunny hillsides and grassy meadows of our interior valleys. The smaller country back roads, like Mountain House Road and Reeves Canyon Road, offer wonderful displays of this beautiful Mariposa Lily.

**What:** A member of the Lily family, *C. vestae* is variable in color. The petals range from white to pink on the outside; on the inside, blotches of deep purple to brown are marked with a band of yellow. It's hard to imagine a flower more beautiful in design and color than the Mariposa Lily.

## (131) Spice Bush – Sweet Shrub *(Calycanthus occidentalis)*, A/S

**When:** The first flowers of Sweet Shrub bloom by mid-May (May–June).

**Where:** Spice Bush loves the moist canyons near streams and small creeks in our wooded foothills. My wife and I always find several beautiful shrubs blooming on Mountain House Road, next to a dry creek bed several miles south of Hopland. The photograph on the opposite page was taken in that location; a wonderful spot to park your car and take a close look at the shrub and its colorful flowers. Other locations where Spice Bush may be found are Highway 128 west of Philo, and Mill Creek Canyon in the Ukiah Valley.

**What:** A member of the Calycanthus family, Spice Bush is a large deciduous shrub, reaching a height of more than eight feet. Its other popular name, Sweet Shrub, comes from the scent of the leaves when crushed, and from the overall fragrance of the plant. The rich color of the Spice Bush flowers and the black urn-shaped seed pods that follow the bloom make this a joy to find in both winter and summer.

## (132) Mariposa Lily *(Calochortus luteus)*, A/S

**When:** *C. luteus* begins to bloom in May (May–June).

**Where:** Yellow Mariposa Lily is found in the same areas where *C. vestae* grows. Along the grassy road banks and meadows of Mountain House Road, you'll find the yellow version of the Mariposa Lily. Mountain House Road provides excellent viewing opportunities, both from the car and on foot.

**What:** *C. luteus* is a member of the Lily Family.

# MAY

**(129) Blue-headed Gilia**

**(130) Mariposa Lily**

**(131) Spice Bush**

**(132) Mariposa Lily**

## (133) Red Ribbons – Clarkia *(Clarkia concinna)*, A/S

**When:** Red Ribbons first appear in early May, and the bloom cycle continues through most of June (April–June).

**Where:** *C. concinna* is found from the coast and inland, in dry wooded foothills and on shaded hillside road banks. Many of our county back roads show lovely concentrations of Red Ribbon. Some of the more beautiful displays of *Clarkia concinna* are found on the rocky banks and walls of Route 175 east of Hopland, and Route 128 south of Boonville.

**What:** A member of the Evening Primrose family, Clarkia is one of our most beautiful wildflowers in shape and coloring. When found blooming on rocky canyon walls and wooded road banks, the deeply cut petals seem to pulsate in lovely shades of pink and red.

## (134) Canyon Dudleya *(Dudleya cymosa)*, A/S

**When:** You'll find the first *D. cymosa* blooming by the middle of May (May–July).

**Where:** Canyon Dudleya is found growing mostly inland from the coast, on rocky outcroppings, cliffs, and canyon walls. Canyon Dudleya is a handsome plant, particularly striking when found in the nooks and crannies of the rocky environment it prefers. You can find *D. cymosa*—usually above eye level—on Mountain House Road, Fish Rock Road, and Low Gap Road.

**What:** A member of the Stonecrop family, Canyon Dudleya's red-to-yellow flowers are set six to twelve inches above a rosette of oval-shaped leaves. Several years ago, while hiking near Low Gap Road, I came upon a stunning display of more than twenty plants that covered a rocky outcropping with their marvelous shape and color.

## (135) Silvia's Daisy *(Tolpis barbata)*, 1½ × A/S

**When:** Silvia's Daisy blooms by early May, and, in scattered areas, will still be with us into late July (May–July).

**Where:** *T. barbata* is locally abundant in dry, open grassy meadows, and in the inland valley foothill areas. Silvia's Daisy may be found in plentiful numbers on the side hills of back roads like Low Gap Road and Mountain House Road.

**What:** Silvia's Daisy is a member of the Aster family. The smallish blossoms have creamy-yellow ray flowers and reddish-brown centers. They grow in scattered masses on stems four to ten inches tall. I'm always surprised to see a few Silvia's Daisies still in bloom in the intense heat of late July and early August.

## (136) Indian Pink *(Silene californica)*, ¾ A/S

**When:** The first flowers of Indian Pink usually appear in late April or early May (April–June).

**Where:** *S. californica* may be found in many different habitats, from the coast to the inner mountains. They seem to prefer shaded, semi-rocky road banks and open woods. Indian Pink likes the woods and shaded grassy hillsides of such roads as Mountain View Road, leading from the coast, and Robinson Creek Road and Mill Creek Canyon Road in the Ukiah valley. In July you'll find Indian Pink in the higher elevations on roads into Anthony Peak and Ham Pass.

**What:** Indian Pink is a member of the Pink family. The brilliant scarlet color and deeply cut petals will draw your attention while you hike the woods or drive the back roads. The name "pink" is derived from the flower's shape, which looks as though cut with pinking shears.

# MAY

**(133) Red Ribbons**

**(134) Canyon Dudleya**

**(135) Silvia's Daisy**

**(136) Indian Pink**

## (137) Ithuriel's Spear – Brodiaea *(Triteleia laxa)*, ½ A/S

**When:** *T. laxa* will bloom during the month of May, along with several other species of *Brodiaea* that are quite similar in appearance (May – July).

**Where:** Ithuriel's Spear is found on grassy hillsides and road banks in full sun or partial shade along many of our back roads from the coast to the inner mountains. Ithuriel's Spear is abundant on the grassy road banks and in the fields along Mountain House Road and Eastside Road.

**What:** *Triteleia laxa* is a member of the Lily family. Only minute differences separate *T. laxa* from several other Brodiaeas that grow in Mendocino County. The flowers of Ithuriel's Spear are funnel-shaped and clustered at the top of one-to-three-foot stems. The color of the flowers varies from pale blue to deep purple. What a welcome sight when you find a few Brodiaeas still in bloom on the dry hillsides in late July.

## (138) Applegate's Paintbrush *(Castilleja applegatei var. martinii)*, A/S

**When:** Depending on elevation and habitat, different species of paintbrush bloom in Mendocino County from early spring into late summer. *C. applegatei* flowers during the late spring and summer (May – July).

**Where:** Applegate's Paintbrush is most often found in the higher elevations of the inner mountains. The flower shown on the opposite page was blooming on a rocky canyon wall along the Eel River, several miles from Dos Rios on Route 162. The flower bracts were back-lit by afternoon light, igniting the plant into a glowing jewel.

**What:** All flowers in the genus Castilleja, which we call "Paintbrush," belong in the Figwort family. In Mendocino County a number of different species of Paintbrush have adapted to environments from the immediate coast to the high peaks of the inner mountains.

## (139) Clustered Broomrape *(Orobanche fasciculata)*, A/S

**When:** Clustered Broomrape will first appear around mid-May if not earlier (April – June).

**Where:** *O. fasciculata* is found growing on coastal bluffs, and inland on dry rocky hills and slopes. We find Clustered Broomrape on the coastal cliffs south of Westport, and inland on the dirt hillside road banks of Highway 253 between Ukiah and Boonville. A large concentration of Broomrape inhabits the rocky cliffs of Ham Pass northeast of Round Valley.

**What:** *O. fasciculata* is a member of the Broomrape family. The flowers feel waxy and are without leaves. Because the plant produces no chlorophyll, it is parasitic, and must rely on a host plant like the roots of Yerba Santa.

## (140) Dannie's Skullcap *(Scutellaria tuberosa)*, 2 × A/S

**When:** Dannie's Skullcap blooms in early May and lasts well into June (May – June).

**Where:** *S. tuberosa* is uncommon, but you'll find it growing in scattered locations on wooded and brushy side hills from the Ukiah Valley to the foothills of the inner mountain range. I find Dannie's Skullcap on the upper trail in Low Gap County Park west of Ukiah.

**What:** Dannie's Skullcap is a low-growing plant that belongs to the Mint family. The small, tubular flowers are solitary and grow from the same axis. The bright purple of the small flower petals contrasts nicely with the brown earth of the wooded slopes where it grows.

# MAY

**(137) Ithuriel's Spear**

**(138) Applegate's Paintbrush**

**(139) Clustered Broomrape**

**(140) Dannie's Skullcap**

## (141) Winter Vetch (Vicia villosa ssp. villosa), 1½ × A/S

**When:** You can expect to see a few Winter Vetch flowers in April, but by May the colorful *V. villosa* will be in full bloom (April–July).

**Where:** Winter Vetch may be found from the coast to the inner mountains. The photograph of a single flower on the opposite page was taken on a grassy hillside on Low Gap Road. A large mass of Winter Vetch had climbed up and over a road bank onto a small hill, blanketing the entire hill in vibrant shades of lilac and purple.

**What:** *V. villosa* (the common name is Vetch) is a member of the Pea family and a native of Europe. At least eleven species of Vetch grow in Mendocino County.

## (142) Hillside Sidalcea – Fringed Sidalcea (Sidalcea diploscypha), A/S

**When:** Hillside Sidalcea is in bloom by late April or early May (April–June).

**Where:** Fringed Sidalcea may be found mostly inland from the coast, growing in grassy fields and meadows, along back roads, and in wooded foothills. Many back roads, like Eastside Road and Mountain House Road, have fine displays of *S. diploscypha*. Some years back, before road banks were groomed or sprayed, there was a remarkable display of Sidalcea along Eastside Road in the Ukiah Valley.

**What:** A member of the Mallow family, Hillside Sidalcea varies in color from pink to deep purple. When found growing in a serpentine environment, it will produce colors of extraordinary intensity.

## (143) Pitcher Sage – Wood-Balm (Lepechinia calycina), A/S

**When:** Pitcher Sage blooms in mid-May (May–July).

**Where:** *L. calycina* is not common in the county, but can be found growing in brush, open slopes, and chaparral. Roads leading to the coast, such as Mountain View Road and Fish Rock Road, contain fine specimens of Wood Balm. Roads east of Highway 101, like the Toll Road out of old Hopland, and the Mayacamas mountain range east of Ukiah, are other areas where you'll find Pitcher Sage.

**What:** A member of the Mint family, Pitcher Sage is a medium-sized shrub that grows three to five feet tall. The wrinkled, leather-like leaves have a distinct aroma. The flowers are urn-shaped and may be either white or pink. The overall effect of Wood-Balm is quite pleasing, particularly on a hot June day with the flowers in bloom and the heavy smell of sage hanging thick in the air.

## (144) Buck Lotus (Lotus crassifolius var. crassifolius), A/S +

**When:** The reddish flower clusters of Buck Lotus are noticeable by the third week in May (May–June).

**Where:** *L. crassifolius* prefers the wooded foothills and chaparral-covered slopes east of Highway 101. Buck Lotus may be found along Route 175 near the Lake County line, and the county road to Lake Pillsbury. The dry, chaparral-covered Mayacamas mountain range east of Ukiah also has scattered displays of Buck Lotus.

**What:** Buck Lotus is a member of the Pea family. It is an irregularly shaped plant up to three feet tall. The flowers are most interesting when the seed vessels swell and elongate, giving the appearance of many small fingers.

# MAY

**(142) Hillside Sidalcea**

**(141) Winter Vetch**

**(143) Pitcher Sage**

**(144) Buck Lotus**

## (145) Firecracker Lily *(Dichelostemma ida-maia)*, A/S

**When:** Firecracker Lily blooms by mid-May (May–June).

**Where:** Firecracker Lily may be found throughout the county, from the coast inland, on grassy road banks and in shady wooded foothills. Many of our back roads, like Orr Springs Road and Mill Creek Canyon Road, offer beautiful displays of Firecracker Lilies. Other areas that host this unique plant are the roads from Laytonville to Dos Rios, and Route 162 to Round Valley and Covelo.

**What:** *D. ida-maia*'s common name, Firecracker Lily, suits this spectacular member of the Lily family. The brilliant red flowers are in clusters resembling firecrackers hanging from stems up to three feet tall. A closer look at the Firecracker Lily will confirm your faith in Nature's incredible diversity in wildflower design.

## (146) Elegant Clarkia *(Clarkia unguiculata)*, 2 × A/S

**When:** Elegant Clarkia begins to bloom in mid-May (May–July).

**Where:** *C. unguiculata* is somewhat rare in our county, but may be found on rocky, shaded road banks and outcroppings. We look for Elegant Clarkia in several locations: along the paved section of the Toll Road, and in Mill Creek Canyon on a steep hillside below the second dam.

**What:** One of several species found in Mendocino County, *C. unguiculata* belongs to the Evening Primrose family. Clarkia will colonize in small groups with numerous flowers climbing stems up to three feet tall. The unusual flower shape and lovely colors of Elegant Clarkia add interesting patterns to the rocky side hills and shaded road banks where it grows.

## (147) Striped Coral-root *(Corallorhiza striata)*, A/S

**When:** Striped Coral-root blooms from late March to early May (April–June).

**Where:** *C. striata* is uncommon in Mendocino county, but may be found at higher foothill elevations (1,200 feet) in moist shaded woods near the coast, and inland east of Highway 101. I always find several plants along Mill Creek Road east of the dams, and on the Toll Road east of Hopland.

**What:** Striped Coral-root is a member of the Orchid family, and grows on stiffly erect stems eight to ten inches tall. When found in shaded woodlands, the many reddish-brown striped flowers give the plant a lovely feathery look. The root, which is a compact mass of rhizomes, may remain dormant for several years, producing no new flowers. Coral-root is a beautiful work of Nature, perfect in its forest setting.

## (148) Mountain Lady's Slipper *(Cypripedium montanum)*, ¾ A/S

**When:** Because of the rarity of the Mountain Lady's Slipper in Mendocino County, it's difficult to give a precise blooming time. The photograph on the opposite page was taken during the last week in May 1994 (May–July).

**Where:** If seen at all, *C. montanum* grows in isolated mixed forests above 2,000 feet. I have seen the Mountain Lady's slipper only once, in the Dakin Preserve, in a partially open wooded glen of mixed fir, tan oak, and madrone. U.S. Forest Service personnel stationed in Covelo in the year 2001 located a small group of *C. montanum* in the inner mountain range southeast of Mendocino Pass.

**What:** One of Nature's masterpieces, *C. montanum* is a member of the Orchid family. Mountain Lady's Slipper is a beautiful, rare flower. A regal-looking plant with one to three flowers that gently hang from stems up to two feet tall, its alternate leaves are oval and deeply veined. If you should happen upon the Lady's Slipper, you've discovered a treasure of the wild—a living token of a time past, when more were to be found and enjoyed.

# MAY

**(145) Firecracker Lily**

**(146) Elegant Clarkia**

**(147) Striped Coral-root**

**(148) Mountain Lady's Slipper**

## (149) White Onion *(Allium amplectens)*, A / S +

**When:** The photograph of White Onion on the opposite page was taken in mid-May (May–June).

**Where:** *A. amplectens* grows inland from the coast on open hills and slopes and dry rocky flats. It's quite common in the county and may be found along such roads as Mountain House Road and Eastside Road. A beautiful colony of White Onion blooms each year on a rocky side hill where Mountain House Road intersects Highway 128.

**What:** At least ten species of *Allium* grow in Mendocino County, all members of the Lily family. When in bloom, *A. amplectens*, like all wild onions, is quite special in shape and color, adding a touch of elegance to the road banks and hillsides where it grows.

## (150) Beaked Tracyina *(Tracyina rostrata)*, 2 × A / S

**When:** Beaked Tracyina begins to bloom during early to mid-May (May–June).

**Where:** *T. rostrata* is very uncommon, and is usually found associated with annual grasses on dryer slopes inland. My wife and I were fortunate to have Kerry Heise, field botanist at the University of California Hopland Research and Extension Center, located east of Hopland, show us where he had found a group of these rare plants. Because of his remarkable discovery and kindness I was able to photograph and include *T. rostrata* in this book.

**What:** Beaked Tracyina is a small, inconspicuous annual in the Aster family. It seldom grows more than a foot tall, with flower heads less than a quarter-inch in diameter. Mixed with annual grasses, *T. rostrata* is extremely difficult to find—even for experienced botanists. Beaked Tracyina occurs only in northwest California, and is known from fewer than a dozen populations. Only two sites have been recorded in Mendocino County.

## (151) Mountain Jewel Flower *(Streptanthus tortuosus var. tortuosus)*, 2 × A / S

**When:** The unusual flowers of Mountain Jewel appear by mid-May (May–July).

**Where:** Mountain Jewel Flower is found above 1,200 feet on the dry, rocky hillsides and outcrops of our inner valley foothills and mountains. Because of their small size, you must look closely to find these plants and their fascinating flowers. Route 253 (the Ukiah–Boonville road), Mountain House Road, and Low Gap Road all sustain excellent specimens of *S. glandulosus*.

**What:** The urn-shaped purple flowers of *S. tortuosus*, a member of the Mustard family, have white markings on the inner edges of the petals. The flowers are assembled along leafless, branched stems one to two feet long, which are covered with bristle-like hairs. The barren-looking stem of Mountain Jewel is host to a beautiful, complex flower that is amazingly intricate in design and shape.

## (152) White Hyacinth – White Brodiaea *(Triteleia hyacinthina)*, A / S

**When:** Look for White Hyacinth, also called White Brodiaea, to bloom during early May (May–June).

**Where:** White Hyacinth is found from the coast to the interior mountains, growing in wet or dry meadows and on open hillside slopes. You'll see White Brodiaea along such back roads as Mountain House Road and the Toll Road. Some years ago I found a large colony of White Hyacinth in a seep spring off Low Gap Road. Covering twenty square yards of a wet meadow, the flowers were so thickly interwoven that they appeared as though planted by human hands.

**What:** White Hyacinth is a member of the Lily family.

# MAY

**(149) White Onion**

**(150) Beaked Tracyina**

**(151) Mountain Jewel Flower**

**(152) White Hyacinth**

## (153) Clintonia (Clintonia andrewsiana), A/S

**When:** Look for the beautiful flowers of Clintonia in early May, with the blooming cycle lasting into mid-June (May–June).

**Where:** Clintonia loves the mixed forests of the coastal region. The deep shade and moist soil of our roadside forests provide excellent areas to see Clintonia. My wife and I find it growing on shaded banks along Orr Springs Road and Cameron Road, several miles inland from the coast.

**What:** The large, polished green leaves of Clintonia are in themselves lovely enough to attract attention; however, when the one-to-two-foot stem suddenly appears with clusters of beautiful, reddish bell-like flowers, Clintonia becomes a true presence in the forest. The distinguished-looking Clintonia adds even more to the forest setting in late August, when the vibrant cobalt-blue berries appear. *C. andrewsiana* is a regal member of the Lily family and a true native of the coastal redwoods.

## (154) Vanilla Leaf – Deer Foot (Achlys triphylla ssp. triphylla), ½ A/S

**When:** The white blossoms of Vanilla Leaf appear by the first week in May (May–July).

**Where:** The light-green leaves of Vanilla Leaf carpet the floor of our coastal forests, moving inland to the edge of the mixed conifer forests west of Highway 101. *A. triphylla* are found in the woodland portions of such back roads as Orr Springs Road and Fish Rock Road, and in Hendy Woods State Park.

**What:** *A. triphylla* is a member of the Barberry family. The unusually shaped leaf has a rounded look: it is composed of three leaflets that are said to resemble the footprint of a deer. The small white flowers grow on a slender stalk that is separate from the leaf stalk, and will rise ten to eighteen inches above the forest floor. Deer Foot is a lovely addition to the understory of our coastal forests.

## (155) Phacelia – Wild Heliotrope (Phacelia bolanderi), A/S

**When:** A number of different species of Phacelia grow in Mendocino County. The photograph on the opposite page was taken on the Greenwood Road in late May (May–July).

**Where:** The species *P. bolanderi* is likely to be found in wooded foothills near the coast, directly on the coast, or on roads leading to it.

**What:** *P. bolanderi* is a member of the Waterleaf family.

## (156) California Huckleberry (Vaccinium ovatum), A/S +

**When:** Look for Huckleberry flowers in early May (May–June).

**Where:** Huckleberry is very common in the redwood forests and brushy slopes and meadows of our coastal regions. The photograph of California Huckleberry flowers on the opposite page was taken on Cameron Road several miles inland from the coast.

**What:** Two species of Huckleberry grow in Mendocino County, both members of the Heath family. *Vaccinium ovatum*, or California Huckleberry, has blue berries that are picked for eating. *Vaccinium parvifolium*, known as Red Huckleberry, has dark-red berries that should not be eaten.

# MAY

**(153) Clintonia**

**(154) Vanilla Leaf**

**(155) Phacelia**

**(156) California Huckleberry**

## (157) Rhododendron – California Rose-Bay *(Rhododendron macrophyllum)*, ½ A/S

**When:** Rhododendron usually reaches peak bloom by mid-May (May–June).

**Where:** Rhododendron is found near the coast in the mixed evergreen woods and pygmy forests just east of Highway 1. The most spectacular specimens are found in and around Mendocino Village and Fort Bragg.

**What:** Rhododendron, also referred to as California Rose-Bay, is a member of the Heath family. In late May, several miles inland from the coast, you'll notice the large pink-to-rose-red flowers of the Rhododendron filling the woods and meadows with breathtaking color. The photograph of the Rose-Bay flower on the opposite page was taken near the coast on Cameron Road, sharing its space with salal, huckleberry, and bear grass.

## (158) Western Azalea *(Rhododendron occidentale)*, ½ A/S

**When:** Western Azalea begins to bloom between mid-May and early June (May–July).

**Where:** The more striking displays of Azalea are found ten or twelve miles inland from the coast, along streams in shaded conifer forests. Beautiful specimens of Azalea the size of small trees may be found growing next to Flynn Creek, along the sides of Flynn Creek Road between Comptche and Highway 128.

**What:** Western Azalea is a member of the Heath family. Azaleas growing along Flynn Creek Road will grow taller than twelve feet. The color of the flowers varies from creamy white to pink with orange centers. Their color and perfume are delightful. Bring along a picnic and spend some time with these native shrubs—you'll marvel at what Nature has created.

## (159) Buckeye *(Aesculus californica)*, A/S

**When:** The long, spike-shaped flowers of Buckeye bloom by mid-May (May–July).

**Where:** The Buckeye tree is found throughout Mendocino County, in wooded foothills, rocky canyons, and open slopes from the coast to the inner mountains. Route 253 from Boonville to Ukiah is an excellent road for Buckeye viewing. Inland, Route 162 toward Mendocino Pass offers marvelous views of our native Buckeye throughout the season.

**What:** One of my favorite trees, *A. californica* is a member of the Buckeye family. The oblong leaves form first, then the flowers, covering the tree in a mantle of pinkish-white color. With Buckeye, you must look quickly, because by late June the flowers are gone and the leaves are starting to brown. They drop by mid-August, leaving the tree bare. You might wonder what manner of tree this is when you see a few leathery pods hanging from the skeletal branches. Finally, in November, the pods open and drop their golden-brown fruit, sewing the seeds of the next generation.

## (160) Western Labrador Tea *(Ledum glandulosum)*, A/S +

**When:** Look for Labrador Tea to bloom by mid-May (May–July).

**Where:** Labrador Tea grows on or near the coast, and is found blooming inland for several miles on roads such as Orr Springs Road, and Little Lake Road near Caspar.

**What:** Labrador Tea is a member of the Heath family. A medium-sized shrub, its outer branches contain clusters of white flowers, with narrow leaves shaped much like miniature Azaleas.

# MAY

**(158) Western Azalea**

**(157) Rhododendron**

**(159) Buckeye**

**(160) Western Labrador Tea**

## (161) Coastal Thrift – Sea Pink *(Armeria maritima)*, A/S +

**When:** Sea Pink will bloom on the coastal headlands by late April or early May (April–July).

**Where:** Sea Pink blooms directly along the coast in the open meadows, headlands, and coastal bluffs. Large masses of Coastal Thrift are found in such areas as the headlands north of Pudding Creek in Fort Bragg, and the Jefferson Way headlands south of Fort Bragg.

**What:** *A. maritima* is a member of the Leadwort family. The flower heads of Sea Pink are rounded, with numerous clusters of small pink flowers growing on stems eight to fourteen inches tall. A coastal breeze will stir Sea Pink into a blur of magenta—a delight to see when mixed with other coastal flowers.

## (162) Rosy Johnny-Tuck *(Triphysaria eriantha ssp. rosea)*, A/S

**When:** Coastal Johnny-Tuck forms carpets of rosy color on the coastal bluffs by mid-May (May–June).

**Where:** You'll find Rosy Johnny-Tuck growing on many of our coastal bluffs and headlands. The maritime bluffs and meadows north of Pudding Creek slough, and the Mendocino Village headlands, are fine places to walk and examine the exquisite colors of coastal Johnny-Tuck.

**What:** Rosy Johnny-Tuck is a member of the Figwort family. Its extremely variable colors range from pink to white. Some of the more eye-catching specimens are found on the Mendocino Village headlands.

## (163) Seaside Daisy *(Erigeron glaucus)*, A/S

**When:** The bright colors of Seaside Daisy are noticeable by early May and will continue to show color well into August (May–Aug.).

**Where:** Seaside Daisy grows only on the coast, and blooms abundantly on many of the coastal cliffs and headlands. Large fields of *Erigeron glaucus* may be found blooming north of Fort Bragg on the Haul Road headlands near Pudding Creek, and on the headlands of Manchester State Park near Alder Creek.

**What:** A member of the Aster family, Seaside Daisy grows in dense masses, producing lovely shades of lavender against the green and gold of the coastal grasses.

## (164) Witch's Teeth *(Lotus formosissimus)*, 2 × A/S

**When:** The bicolored flowers of Witch's Teeth begin blooming by mid-May (May–July).

**Where:** Witch's Teeth grow primarily on the coast, in the meadows and on the headlands along Highway 1. Witch's Teeth makes a fine showing south of Fort Bragg on the Jefferson Way headlands, and in the barrens east of Mendocino Village.

**What:** An attractive member of the Pea family, Witch's Teeth are low-growing plants, quite visible and easy to identify. The banner petal is yellow; the two lower petals are pink to purple and are arranged like rows of teeth. I often wonder how some wildflowers come by their common names, but in the case of Witch's Teeth the name applies.

# MAY

**(161) Coastal Thrift**

**(162) Rosy Johnny-Tuck**

**(163) Seaside Daisy**

**(164) Witch's Teeth**

## (165) Twinberry *(Lonicera involucrata)*, 2 × A / S

**When:** The Twinberry shrub will bloom by mid-April or early in May (April–July).

**Where:** Twinberry grows in moist places along the coast, and less frequently inland in wooded foothills near streams and seeps. Nearly all of the *L. involucrata* that we find is on or near the coast, on roads similar to the Branscomb Road north of Westport, and Miner Hole Road north of Pt. Arena. Elk Creek Basin south of Elk supports fine specimens of Twinberry and other flowering shrubs.

**What:** A member of the Honeysuckle family, *L. involucrata* is a medium-to-large shrub up to ten feet in height. Twinberry has a number of twin red-to-yellow flowers that protrude from the axis of the main stem and leaf. After the flowers bloom, Twinberry becomes more noticeable when two beautiful, shiny black berries form, held in place by brilliant red bracts.

## (166) Beach Morning Glory *(Calystegia soldanella)*, A / S

**When:** Beach Morning Glory blooms from late April well into July (April–July).

**Where:** *C. soldanella* is found directly on the coast, growing on sand dunes and sand hills. You'll find Beach Morning Glory blooming on the dunes of Manchester Beach State Park, along with many other interesting shore plants.

**What:** A member of the Morning Glory family, *C. soldanella* is an attractive plant. Its deep-green kidney-shaped leaves and lovely pink trumpet-shaped flowers contrast handsomely against the color of the coastal sandhills and dunes.

## (167) Salal *(Gaultheria shallon)*, 2 × A / S

**When:** The small urn-shaped flowers of Salal are noticeable by early May (May–July).

**Where:** Salal is found along the coastal headlands, and inland among the redwoods and forest openings where huckleberry and rhododendron grow. Many of our back roads leading to the coast, such as Fish Rock Road, Cameron Road, and Highway 20, are excellent areas for viewing Salal.

**What:** *G. shallon* is a member of the Heath family. The leathery green leaves and urn-shaped flowers of Salal form dense thickets of small shrub-like plants on our windswept coastline. Where the coastal winds are no longer a factor, the inland version of Salal becomes larger and more open-branched, allowing the shrub greater freedom to spread.

## (168) Cow Parsnip *(Heracleum lanatum)*, ¼ A / S

**When:** Cow Parsnips bloom in mid-April, and reach peak bloom by late May (April–July).

**Where:** Although *H. lanatum* may be found inland, seeking out moist seeps and shady canyon creeks, it is largely a coastal plant. Cow Parsnips form large colonies in areas like the coastal headlands and meadows south of Westport, and along the moist road banks of Mountain View Road as it nears the coast.

**What:** A large, robust plant, *H. lanatum* is a member of the Carrot family. The large, maple-like leaves are often one to two feet across; the many rounded flower heads form a large attractive umbel, all supported on thick hollow stems reaching heights greater than five feet. We counted more than 200 Cow Parsnips on a coastal hillside several miles south of Westport—a most impressive sight.

# MAY

**(165) Twinberry**

**(166) Beach Morning Glory**

**(167) Salal**

**(168) Cow Parsnip**

## (169) Sidalcea *(Sidalcea malvaeflora)*, A/S

**When:** Sidalcea blooms during the early part of May (May–July).

**Where:** *S. malvaeflora* is found along the coastal headlands and ocean bluffs, and, to a lesser degree, inland in open meadows and on grassy hillsides. Sidalcea forms lovely carpets of color on the bluffs and headlands of both Manchester Beach State Park and along the Haul Road north of Fort Bragg.

**What:** A member of the Mallow family, *S. malvaeflora* is one of several species of Sidalcea found in the county. With its magnificent pink-to-magenta coloring, Sidalcea in bloom is a remarkable sight.

## (170) Calla Lily *(Zantedeschia aethiopica)*, ½ A/S

**When:** The cycle of bloom for Calla Lilies may last four or five months. I've chosen the month of May as prime time for viewing the Calla Lily, particularly along the coast (March–Sept.).

**Where:** Calla Lilies grow along the entire length of our coast, seeking out the wet canyons and seeps found on the ocean bluffs and headlands. Years ago, next to Highway 1, my wife and I spotted a great mass of *Z. aethiopica* blooming along a fence line that followed a canyon up into the mountains. For years we've tried to find this same location, but without luck. We keep hoping to find the spot and put it on film so other people can enjoy what was truly an amazing sight.

**What:** *Z. aethiopica* is a member of the Arum family. Calla Lily is a garden escapee that has done extremely well in the wild coastal regions of our county. I've included it in this book for the great pleasure it gives people.

## (171) Sea Fig *(Carpobrotus chilensis)*, A/S

**When:** The bright, rose-colored flowers of Sea Fig first appear in late March and early April, and remain in evidence through most of the summer (May–Sept.).

**Where:** Sea Fig is strictly a coastal plant, found on the headlands and sand dunes along much of our coastline. Beautiful examples of Sea Fig may be seen on the ocean bluffs and dunes north of Fort Bragg, and south in Manchester Beach State Park.

**What:** *C. chilensis* is a member of the Fig-Marigold family. Another species is the Hottentot Fig; both species were introduced to stabilize the coastal sand dunes.

## (172) Mahonia – Oregon-Grape – Barberry *(Berberis nervosa)*, A/S

**When:** You'll find Oregon Grape blooming in late April or early May (May–June).

**Where:** Oregon Grape, also called Longleaf Berberis, is more commonly found in the coastal forests, but may also be seen to the east in the wooded foothills of the inner mountains. I find dense masses of coastal Oregon Grape in the mixed conifers around the Caspar Cemetery, and scattered plants in Van Damme State Park and along Fish Rock Road.

**What:** *B. nervosa* is a member of the Barberry family. Several species of Barberry grow in Mendocino County. *B. nervosa* is a robust plant that can grow several feet tall. Its spike-shaped yellow flowers and long, holly-like leaves make Barberry an attractive addition to any garden.

**(169) Sidalcea**

**(170) Calla Lily**

**(171) Sea Fig**

**(172) Mahonia**

## (173) Youth-on-Age – Pig-a-back Plant *(Tolmiea menziesii)*, 2 × A/S

**When:** You can expect to see the unusual-looking flowers of Youth-on-Age in early May (May–July).

**Where:** *T. menziesii* is found in the cool moist seeps and canyons of our evergreen coastal forests, and less frequently in the higher elevations of the inner mountains. Although not plentiful in Mendocino County, we enjoy looking for and finding Youth-on-Age in Russian Gulch State Park and along Highway 128 as it follows the Navarro River coastward. *T. menziesii* is found from Alaska to central California.

**What:** A member of the Saxifrage family, *T. menziesii* is a most interesting plant. The many stems are formed from buds at the base of the leaf blade, producing a bouquet of odd-looking flowers. The plant is also given the common name Pig-a-back because, as the old leaves drop, the new leaves that form at the base of the old ones ride to the ground, taking root to begin a new growing cycle. The photograph on the opposite page will give you some idea of the intricate flower design of the Pig-a-back plant.

## (174) Thimbleberry *(Rubus parviflorus)*, A/S

**When:** The flowers of the Thimbleberry shrub bloom in late April or early May. The cycle of bloom continues through the summer months (May-Aug.).

**Where:** Thimbleberry is most noticeable in the moist woods and seeps of our coastal redwoods, and less common in the mixed forests of the inner mountains. Areas such as Old River Road along the Gualala River, and state parks such as Van Damme and Russian Gulch show fine displays of Thimbleberry.

**What:** A member of the Rose family, *R. parviflorus* is a medium-to-large shrub. Its maple-like leaves support a scattering of white flowers crinkled at the edges like old lace. Bright-red berries, much like raspberries in shape and texture, form after the flowers have bloomed. *R. parviflorus* is a handsome shrub that mixes well with the other coastal forest plants.

## (175) Dwarf Brodiaea – Ground Brodiaea *(Brodiaea terrestris)*, A/S +

**When:** Ground Brodiaea should bloom by early May (May–July).

**Where:** The lovely Ground Brodiaea is found from the coast inland, in grassy meadows and fields. I have more luck finding this elegant Brodiaea in such areas as the Jefferson Way headlands south of Fort Bragg.

**What:** A member of the Lily family, *B. terrestris* grows very close to the ground on stems less than an inch tall. For a closer look at the rare blue-to-violet colors of Ground Brodiaea, you'll have to assume a crawling position.

## (176) Fringe Cups *(Tellima grandiflora)*, A/S +

**When:** The first Fringe Cups will bloom by mid-May (May–July).

**Where:** Fringe Cups grow in the moist redwoods and mixed forests of our coastal regions. *T. grandiflora* may be found in such areas as Russian Gulch State Park and along Highway 1 in the Elk Creek basin.

**What:** *T. grandiflora* is a member of the Saxifrage family. The flowers are red-tipped and arranged along hairy stems up to three feet tall. The leaves are maple-like in appearance, and the flowers quite small. To fully appreciate the flower design of Fringe Cups, move in for a closer look.

# MAY

**(173) Youth-on-Age**

**(174) Thimbleberry**

**(175) Dwarf Brodiaea**

**(176) Fringe Cups**

## (177) Coastal Onion – Magenta Wild Onion *(Allium dichlamydeum)*, A/S

**When:** Magenta Wild Onion blooms during the latter part of May (May – July).

**Where:** *A. dichlamydeum* is a coastal plant that grows on the cliffs and bluffs of our ocean headlands. You'll find Coastal Onion on the headlands north of Pudding Creek slough, and in the coastal meadows of Jefferson Way south of Fort Bragg.

**What:** A member of the Lily family, *A. dichlamydeum*, with its lovely magenta hue, adds a new dimension in color to the other coastal flowers. The umbel-shaped flower head consists of many small blossoms that rest at the top of stems three to five inches tall. Magenta Wild Onion colonizes into small groups that are easy to find and identify among the other flowers of the coastal headlands.

## (178) Coastal Poppy *(Eschscholzia californica)*, A/S

**When:** Poppies that flourish along the coast may be found almost throughout the year. On the coast, May is a very good month for Poppies. (May – )

**Where:** You'll see Poppies almost anywhere along the coast. I particularly enjoy finding them on the stable dunes of Manchester Beach State Park, and Ten Mile north of Fort Bragg.

**What:** A member of the Poppy family, I've included the ocean-side version (see photograph #17, page 20 for inner valley) because of the variety of colors and shapes it displays in its coastal environment.

## (179) Yellow Sand Verbena *(Abronia latifolia)*, A/S +

**When:** Yellow Sand Verbena has a long blooming cycle: more than four months, with the early bloom arriving in May (May – Aug.).

**Where:** *A. latifolia* loves coastal sand hills, dunes, and beaches. Among the places you can find Yellow Sand Verbena are the sand dunes of Manchester State Park, and along the sandy beach of Big River.

**What:** Yellow Sand Verbena is a member of the Four-o'clock family. The succulent kidney-shaped leaves lie beneath numerous yellow tubular flowers in the form of an umbel. The root system and stalk of *A. latifolia* is said to exceed four feet in length, allowing the plant to bloom successfully in the continually shifting sands.

## (180) Bead Lily – False Lily of The Valley *(Maianthemum dilatatum)*, A/S +

**When:** The early flowers of the Bead Lily bloom by mid-May (May – July).

**Where:** False Lily of The Valley is found growing on or near the coast, in wet, boggy terrain, often in moist, shady woods. Look for the Bead Lily in places like MacKerricher State Park and the entrance to Jefferson Way headlands.

**What:** Bead Lily is a member of the Lily family. The Bead Lily's small white flowers are cupped by its deeply veined, heart-shaped leaves, forming thick carpets of green against the boggy soil.

# MAY

**(177) Coastal Onion**

**(178) Coastal Poppy**

**(179) Yellow Sand Verbena**

**(180) Bead Lily**

## (181) Mendocino Paintbrush (Castilleja mendocinensis), A/S

**When:** You can expect to see the beautiful Mendocino Paintbrush in bloom by early May (May–July).

**Where:** *C. mendocinensis* is indigenous to the coastlines of Mendocino and Humboldt Counties. Because Mendocino Paintbrush grows in a limited area, the California Native Plant Society considers it rare throughout its range in California. It is also a candidate for federal listing as an endangered species. Stunning displays of Mendocino Paintbrush may be seen on the coastal headlands of the Haul Road north of Fort Bragg, and south on the windswept ocean bluffs of Manchester Beach State Park near Alder Creek.

**What:** *C. mendocinensis* is a member of the Figwort family. The incandescent hue of Mendocino Paintbrush ranges from scarlet to orange-red, producing a color show unparalleled in beauty. The bluffs and headlands of Mendocino County offer an outstanding opportunity to view the rare and lovely *C. mendocinensis*.

## (182) Dudleya Farinosa – Powdery Dudleya (Dudleya farinosa), ½ A/S

**When:** *D. Farinosa* blooms by the third week in May (May–July).

**Where:** Powdery Dudleya is found only on the cliffs and bluffs of our coastal headlands. A turnout for cars—part of old Highway 1—several miles south of Pt. Arena and a little beyond Schooner Gulch is a safe place to park and look for *D. Farinosa* and other coastal plants. This area also provides an excellent view of Bowling Ball Beach to the north, and is a great location for watching migrating whales.

**What:** Powdery Dudleya is a member of the Stonecrop family. A thick stem more than six inches tall supports the yellow flowers, with the rosette leaves at the base covered with a mealy white powder.

## (183) Common Hedge Nettle (Stachys ajugoides var. rigida), A/S

**When:** Common Hedge Nettle begins blooming in late April or early May (May–Aug.).

**Where:** The species *Stachys ajugoides var. rigida* is found abundantly from the coast, in coastal thickets and shrubs, to the wooded foothills of the inner valleys. The more striking specimens are found in coastal areas like Miner Hole Road north of Pt. Arena, and Chadburn Gulch south of Westport.

**What:** A member of the Mint family, Common Hedge Nettle is variable in growth and appearance depending on the habitat. Hedge Nettle is almost always light rose to purple in color.

## (184) Coastal Bush Lupine – Yellow Bush Lupine (Lupinus arboreus), A/S

**When:** Coastal Bush Lupine has a long blooming span, and can be seen flowering from late May to early August (May–Aug.).

**Where:** *L. arboreus* grows along the coastal bluffs and headlands from Gualala north to Sinkyone. Large thickets of Coastal Bush Lupine are found in Manchester Beach State Park and Russian Gulch State Park.

**What:** A member of the Pea family, Coastal Bush Lupine will grow into medium-sized shrubs more than four feet tall. Silvery-gray leaves highlight the blue or creamy-yellow flowers, giving the shrub a clean, pleasing look. The photograph on the opposite page was taken near Gualala.

# MAY

**(181) Mendocino Paintbrush**

**(182) Dudleya Farinosa**

**(183) Common Hedge Nettle**

**(184) Coastal Bush Lupine**

## (185) Sugar Scoop – Lace Flower *(Tiarella trifoliata var. unifoliata)*, A/S

**When:** The flowers of *T. trifoliata* become noticeable by early May (May–Aug.).

**Where:** Sugar Scoop, or Lace Flower, is found in the moist redwood and evergreen forests from the coast inland to Highway 101. You'll find this charming little plant in many areas, among them the Gualala River Road, Faulkner County Park west of Boonville, and Admiral Wm. H. Standley State Recreation Area just east of Branscomb.

**What:** A member of the Saxifrage family, Lace Flower is a delightful plant of our coastal forests. The tiny flowers are star-shaped, with long stamens crowning the one-to two-foot plant. The leaves are divided into three leaflets with toothed margins.

## (186) Coastal Iris – Douglas Iris *(Iris douglasiana)*, ¾ A/S

**When:** The coastal version of Douglas Iris may bloom as early as late February. Because of the wide habitat *I. douglasiana* enjoys, you'll find it blooming in the foothills and inner mountains during the summer months, and on the coast from March through July. I choose the headlands along the coast in May as the peak bloom for Douglas Iris (March–Aug.).

**Where:** *I. douglasiana* grows throughout Mendocino County, from the coast inland to the inner mountain ranges. The headlands above Alder Creek, at the north end of Manchester Beach State Park, provide a wonderful place to see Douglas Iris and other coastal wildflowers in prime bloom. Those headlands also offer a visual sweep of open prairie and beach that is unmatched in beauty and scope.

**What:** A member of the Iris family, Douglas Iris is a royal beauty, ranging in color from deep purple to creamy white. It reaches perfection when seen in great colonies along the coastal headlands.

## (187) Bee Plant *(Scrophularia californica)*, 2 × A/S

**When:** The California Bee Plant's flowering cycle starts in March and lasts into August. I've listed mid-May as the peak blooming time for *S. californica* (April–June).

**Where:** Bee Plant is commonly found near the coast, but may also be found in the wooded foothills of the inner valleys. On the coast, Highway 1 provides some excellent areas to view *S. californica*, particularly between Elk and Manchester.

**What:** A member of the Figwort family, the Bee Plant is a shrub that grows to five feet. The small, reddish flowers are perfect storage capsules for the abundant nectar they produce, thereby attracting bees throughout the spring and summer.

## (188) Coast Lily *(Lilium maritimum)*, A/S +

**When:** The Coast Lily begins blooming about the third week in May (May–July).

**Where:** Coast Lily grows near the coast in areas of mixed brush, huckleberry, and open woods. You'll find the Coast Lily on such roads as Cameron Road and Little Lake Road, several miles inland from the coast.

**What:** *L. maritimum* is a member of the Lily family. It grows to a height of three feet, with as many as six bell-shaped flowers dispersed along the stem. The deep, rich reds of the Coast Lily are among the most amazing in the spectrum. The photograph of the Coast Lily on the opposite page was taken on Cameron Road, in a brushy open flat where huckleberry, rhododendron, and juniper abound.

# MAY

**(185) Sugar Scoop**

**(186) Coastal Iris**

**(187) Bee Plant**

**(188) Coast Lily**

## (189) Ox Eye Daisy *(Leucanthemum vulgare)*, A/S

**When:** Ox Eye Daisy blooms in early May, with the flowering cycle lasting well into summer (May – Aug.).

**Where:** Ox Eye Daisy is found from the coast to the inner mountain range. Common to the coast, it also grows in large clusters along many of our back roads. Elk Greenwood Road and Highway 1 north of Westport have large displays of *L. vulgare*.

**What:** A member of the Sunflower family, Ox Eye Daisy is a native of Europe. During the early summer months, Ox Eye Daisy in cheerful full bloom may be seen brightening many of our back roads.

## (190) Cream Bush – Ocean Spray *(Holodiscus discolor var. discolor)*, A/S

**When:** The first sprays of Cream Bush flowers appear by late May and reach full bloom by mid-June  (May – July).

**Where:** Ocean Spray, usually identified as a coastal plant, is also found inland in the wooded foothills and slopes of our inner mountains. Coastal Cream Bush is at its best along Highway 1 between Big River and Manchester, and along Highway 128 several miles inland from the coast.

**What:** A member of the Rose family, Cream Bush is a large shrub that has plumes of small white-to-brownish flowers that cascade down the plant, creating a foam-like appearance. With its maple-like leaves and clusters of cascading flowers, Cream Bush is a shrub with a beautiful feathery quality that's hard to ignore. The clusters of small flowers carry a slight vanilla scent that delights the nose.

## (191) Inside-Out Flower *(Vancouveria planipetala)*, A/S

**When:** The first Inside-Out Flowers bloom about mid-May (May – July).

**Where:** *V. planipetala*, or Inside-Out Flower, is commonly found in the mixed forests and woods of our coastal regions and inland to Highway 101. Many of the back roads that lead through wooded foothills and redwoods support fine specimens of the Inside-Out Flower. The photograph of *V. planipetala* on the opposite page was taken in Admiral Wm. H. Standley State Recreation Area, east of the town of Branscomb.

**What:** A member of the Barberry family, Inside-Out Flower is quite distinctive, because the small flower petals are swept backward, as if inside out. The shiny green leaves are squarish in shape.

## (192) Foxglove *(Digitalis purpurea)*, A/S

**When:** Foxglove makes its appearance around mid-May (May – July).

**Where:** Foxglove is partial to the coast, but may also be found inland in moist, shady woods near creeks and streams, and in open, wet meadows. Sizable concentrations of Foxglove are found along Highway 1 north of Rockport and in the meadows of Usal State Park.

**What:** A member of the Figwort family, Foxglove is another native of Europe. *D. purpurea* is well established in the Pacific Northwest. While traveling into the Kalmiopsis Wilderness in Southern Oregon, my wife and I came upon an entire mountain meadow covered with Foxglove, an incredible vision of pure color that I will never forget. Although Foxglove is not native to our country, I include it in this book because it now belongs here, adding color and beauty to the many areas where it abounds.

# MAY

**(189) Ox Eye Daisy**

**(190) Cream Bush**

**(191) Inside-Out Flower**

**(192) Foxglove**

# JUNE

By the early part of June, Mendocino County has been transformed. The inland valleys have turned from green to a rich golden brown. The native oaks, with their beautiful, dark olive-colored leaves and black trunks, stand out against the golden hills as solitary sentinels waiting for the heat that is sure to come. The inner coastal mountains look refreshed from the snow and rain they received during the winter. Spring has arrived in the higher elevations, and a whole new cycle of mountain flowers is starting to bloom. Along the coast, the headlands are rich with wildflower color and will remain so for several months. The coastal redwoods gather moisture from the ocean fog drawn inland by the valley heat. Summer has arrived, and the great flower display of our meadows and hillsides is ending, but don't despair—we are about to receive more lovely gifts from Nature. The exotic mountain flowers of the deep woods are to be found in the higher elevations, along with the Mariposa Lilies that still linger on our grassy hillsides. The beautiful Tiger and Redwood Lilies waiting patiently to go onstage will soon make their first appearance; certainly, this must fascinate and delight you.

## (193) Gnome Plant – Pink Asparagus *(Hemitomes congestum)*, A/S

**When:** Although it's difficult to predict precisely when Gnome Plants will bloom, I consider the early part of June the most likely (June–Aug.).

**Where:** Pink asparagus is rare in Mendocino County, and grows mainly in the rich soil and humus of the coastal forests. My wife and I once saw Gnome Plants blooming in the mixed forests of Brooktrails, where the photograph on the opposite page was taken several years ago, off Ridge Road near Goose Lane. *H. congestum* is listed as endemic to the mixed conifer forests of the North Coast, Klamath, and Cascade Mountains, and the High Sierra Nevada to British Columbia.

**What:** *H. congestum* is a member of the Heath family. The small, fleshy pink flowers of Gnome Plants grow in little clusters from a mass of fibrous roots. It's hard to find these plants in the deep woods, as they grow close to the ground and are difficult to see in the forest dusk.

## (194) Small Ground Cone *(Boschniakia strobilacea)*, A/S

**When:** The blooming time of Ground Cones is somewhat unpredictable; however, you should find some early bloomers around the first part of June (June–July).

**Where:** Ground Cones are found inland from the coast in mixed forests of redwood, fir, and tan oak, and on occasion in chaparral-covered foothills. The photograph on the opposite page was taken in Brooktrails in a heavily wooded flat off Ridge Road.

**What:** *B. strobilacea* is a member of the Broomrape family. Small Ground Cones are parasitic and need a host to survive. The most likely hosts are the roots of trees such as madrone and redwood. From a distance, Ground Cones appear like pinecones that grow directly from the forest floor.

## (195) Sugarstick – Candystick *(Allotropa virgata)*, A/S

**When:** The first Sugarsticks appear in late May or early June (June–July).

**Where:** Although somewhat rare in our county, Candysticks may be found in the deep woods of mixed conifers and hardwoods growing from the forest duff. My wife and I find Candysticks growing above eye level along the wooded banks of Mountain View Road, and in the higher elevations of Brooktrails' mixed forests.

**What:** Sugarsticks are members of the Heath family. *A. virgata* is striped like a candy stick, and flourishes in small groups of three to five, with some plants reaching a height of two feet. Unusual looking, Sugarsticks are considered to be saprophytic (they take their nourishment from the dead vegetable matter found on the forest floor).

## (196) Pinesap *(Monotropa hypopithys)*, A/S

**When:** It's not easy to say precisely when Pinesap will bloom, but if you start looking around the middle of June you might be in luck (June–July).

**Where:** Pinesap is a rare plant that seeks out the deep forests of tan oak, fir, and redwoods near the coast. The photograph of *M. hypopithys* on the opposite page, showing a cluster of waxy white flowers on a single stem, was taken in the higher elevations of Brooktrails.

**What:** A member of the Heath family, Pinesap is a saprophyte, feeding on decaying leaves and forest material.

# JUNE

**(193) Gnome Plant**

**(194) Small Ground Cone**

**(195) Sugarstick**

**(196) Pinesap**

## (197) California Lady's Slipper *(Cypripedium californicum)*, ¾ A/S

**When:** You'll need luck to find the California Lady's Slipper; if you find it, chances are it will be during late May or early June (May–June).

**Where:** I've never seen California Lady's Slipper growing in Mendocino County; however, in 2001, U.S. Forest Service personnel located a small colony off of the Blands Cove Road in the northwest section of the inner mountain range. Normally found below 5,000 feet, its preferred habitat is the wet rocky margins of streams, and the moist, shady canyons of hidden forest glens. I've talked to old-timers who claim to have found Lady's Slipper along Tomki creek on the Tomki Road, and in the Hearst area farther north. I photographed the Lady's Slippers on the opposite page in the Kalmiopsis Wilderness of southwestern Oregon on June 12, 1992, during a snowstorm (that's another story).

**What:** A member of the Orchid family, *C. californicum* is extremely rare in Mendocino County. If found it should not be disturbed, but left alone in quiet solitude.

## (198) White-veined Wintergreen *(Pyrola picta)*, A/S

**When:** You can expect to see the first Pyrola blooming by late June (June–July).

**Where:** *P. picta* is a woodland plant, and is found in shaded forests of mixed species at elevations above 2,000 feet. Beautiful specimens of White-veined Wintergreen may be seen blooming in Brooktrails, off Ridge Road west of Willits. This plant is sometimes leafless, variable, and may hybridize with other species.

**What:** *P. picta* is a member of the Heath family. The photograph on the opposite page is of the leafless variety. The oval, white-veined leaves of *P. picta* identify this plant, as do its flowers—waxy to the touch—and its pink-to-greenish-yellow petals.

## (199) Mountain Morning Glory – Hill Morning Glory *(Calystegia subacaulis)*, A/S

**When:** Mountain Morning Glory blooms during early April in lower elevations and continues through June at elevations above 3,000 feet (April–June).

**Where:** *C. subacaulis* is attracted to hilly mountainous areas and is partial to a serpentine environment. Rocky slopes in such regions as Low Gap and, farther east, Hull Mountain and Mendocino Pass, sustain fine samplings of Mountain Morning Glory.

**What:** Hill Morning Glory is a lovely member of the Morning Glory family. *C. subacaulis*, with its cream-colored petals tinted slightly purple, offers an attractive presence that deserves your close inspection.

## (200) Fimbriate Pinesap *(Pleuricospora fimbriolata)*, ¾ A/S

**When:** From the only contact I've had with Fimbriate Pinesap, I have to list mid-June or early July as the likely bloom time (June–July).

**Where:** Fimbriate Pinesap grows randomly in deep forest duff in the mixed conifer forests on or near the coast. I took the photograph on the opposite page in Brooktrails, in a mixed forest of redwood, fir, and tan oak.

**What:** Uncommon in Mendocino County, *Pleuricospora fimbriolata* is believed to be saprophytic, producing no chlorophyll of its own, but living on dead organic material in the soil. Fimbriate Pinesap is a member of the Heath family.

# JUNE

**(197) California Lady's Slipper**

**(198) White-veined Wintergreen**

**(199) Mountain Morning Glory**

**(200) Fimbriate Pinesap**

## (201) Stream Orchid *(Epipactis gigantea)*, 1¼ × A / S

**When:** Stream Orchids reach their peak bloom in early June (June–July).

**Where:** *E. gigantea* is found in grassy or sandy gravel banks of rivers, streams, and small creeks. Look in such places as the Eel River northeast of Potter Valley, and the Navarro River near the town of Philo. The photograph on the opposite page was taken on the Old Toll Road near Highland Springs Dam in Lake County.

**What:** *E. gigantea* is member of the Orchid family. Stream Orchids grow in dense colonies. Their small flowers, mostly hidden by the narrow, deeply veined leaves, are difficult to spot.

## (202) Wavy-Leaf Soap Plant *(Chlorogalum pomeridianum)*, A / S

**When:** Look for Wavy-Leaf Soap plant to bloom in late May or early June (June–July).

**Where:** *C. pomeridianum* grows on open grassy hillsides and road banks from the coast to the interior valley. Wavy-Leaf Soap Plant is abundant on such back roads as Eastside Road between Hopland and Ukiah, and Mountain House Road.

**What:** A member of the Lily family, Wavy-Leaf Soap Plant has some unique and unusual qualities that are quite interesting. The Soap Plant may grow to a height of five feet on a thick stem supporting numerous twig-like branches that are barren of leaves. If you look at the base of the plant, however, you'll see a large rosette of wavy green leaves. Flowers bloom on the leafless branches only in the late afternoon and early evening, and from a distance look like puffs of wispy cotton. When *C. pomeridianum* blooms, it's time to stop and take a close look at the delicate beauty of the flowers. Early Native Americans rendered the bulb of the Wavy-Leaf Soap Plant edible by roasting it; the bulb was also a good substitute for soap.

## (203) Woodland Madia *(Madia madioides)*, A / S

**When:** Woodland Madia blooms during the summer months, from late April through July (April–July).

**Where:** *M. madioides* is found from the coast to the foothill woodlands of the inner valleys. I usually see it in woodland areas along such roads as Low Gap Road, Mill Creek Road, and Orr Springs Road.

**What:** Woodland Madia is a member of the Aster family. A somewhat solitary plant, it adds color and grace to the dry summer woodlands and coastal areas it inhabits.

## (204) Mountain Mahogany *(Cercocarpus betuloides var. betuloides)*, A / S

**When:** Mountain Mahogany's bright silver, needle-shaped seed pods become quite evident by early June (June–July).

**Where:** The species of Mountain Mahogany, known as Birch Leaf Mountain Mahogany, inhabits our woodland and chaparral-covered foothills and mountain slopes. You'll find Cercocarpus on such back roads as Low Gap Road, Robinson Creek Road, and Route 162 to Covelo.

**What:** A large shrub, *C. betuloides* is most strikingly noticeable in late June or early July, when the inconspicuous needle-shaped flowers have turned to fruit, forming long plumes of feathery silver. Birch Leaf Mountain Mahogany is a member of the Rose family.

# JUNE

**(201) Stream Orchid**

**(202) Wavy-Leaf Soap Plant**

**(203) Woodland Madia**

**(204) Mountain Mahogany**

## (205) Alum-Root *(Heuchera micrantha)*, ¼ A/S

**When:** Alum-Root starts its flowering cycle in late May and reaches full bloom by mid-June (May–July).

**Where:** Look for Alum-Root on moist canyon walls and rocky outcrops of wet humus and moss. Some of the more noticeable displays are found on Fish Rock Road and the Old Toll Road.

**What:** Alum-Root is a member of the Saxifrage family. The flowers are small and numerous, with maple-like leaves growing at the base. The overall effect of Alum-Root is quite airy and pleasing when seen growing on shady banks and moss-covered rocks.

## (206) Venus Thistle *(Cirsium occidentale var. venustum)*, A/S

**When:** *Cirsium occidentale* becomes noticeable by early to mid-June (June–Aug.).

**Where:** Venus Thistle is common throughout the county, and is found in wooded foothills, on rocky cliffs, and in the dry meadows and forests of the inner coastal mountain range. A number of lovely Red Venus Thistles adorn the rocky cliffs of the Boonville grade and Low Gap Road.

**What:** Venus Thistle is a member of the Aster family, varying in color from crimson to pink and sometimes white. *C. occidentale* is a handsome plant that brightens up our rocky hillsides and road banks during the summer months.

## (207) Yerba Santa *(Eriodictyon californicum)*, A/S

**When:** The Yerba Santa shrub is in full bloom by late May or early June (May–July).

**Where:** A common shrub of chaparral, large patches of Yerba Santa may be found on the dry rocky slopes and hillsides of our interior valleys and foothills. Dense thickets of Yerba Santa grow along Low Gap Road and Pine Mountain Road west of Ukiah.

**What:** A member of the Waterleaf family, *E. californicum* is a large shrub. Its numerous white flowers are funnel-shaped, with bitter-tasting aromatic leaves. In early days, the leaves of Yerba Santa were prized as a remedy for colds.

## (208) Wild Honeysuckle *(Lonicera hispidula)*, A/S

**When:** When mid-June arrives, so do the flowers of the Honeysuckle vine (June–Aug.).

**Where:** Honeysuckle may be found growing from the coast to the mixed woods and foothills of our interior valleys. The photograph on the opposite page was taken on Low Gap Road.

**What:** *L. hispidula* is a member of the Honeysuckle family. Wild Honeysuckle is a woody vine that loves to climb, twining itself around shrubs and small trees in such a way that you catch only an occasional glimpse of its pink-to-red flowers. In the fall, the translucent red berries hang in clusters, reminding us of the approaching winter.

# JUNE

**(205) Alum-Root**

**(206) Venus Thistle**

**(207) Yerba Santa**

**(208) Wild Honeysuckle**

## (209) Seep-Willow – Baccharis *(Baccharis salicifolia)*, A/S

**When:** The early bloom of Seep Willow occurs around mid-July and continues well into September (July – Sept.).

**Where:** Baccharis forms large thickets, nearly always growing near drying creeks, streams, and moist seeps. A thick growth blooms in Low Gap County Park next to a small vernal pool. Seep-Willow may be found on such back roads as Orr Springs Road and the Branscomb – Laytonville Road.

**What:** A member of the Aster family, Seep Willow forms dense thickets of willow-like stems reaching heights of more than five feet. The numerous, small, button-like flowers are branched at the top of the stems. Although not overly attractive on its own, Baccharis lends a sense of enhancement and completion to the watersheds and moist seeps where it lives.

## (210) Malacothrix *(Malacothrix floccifera)*, A/S

**When:** *M. Floccifera* likes the heat of the summer months. You'll see the first ones blooming by mid-May (June – July).

**Where:** Most of the Malacothrix that my wife and I have found grows on dry road banks and rocky slopes from our inland valley areas to the inner mountains. The most noticeable and abundant ones live on Low Gap Road and Fish Rock Road, and, farther east, on Route 162 between Dos Rios and Round Valley.

**What:** A member of the Aster family, *M. floccifera* shouldn't be ignored. It grows to a height of two feet; the petals of its beautifully designed flowers are usually white, but sometimes tinged pink, and the undersides are almost always marked with pink stripes. Except for the basal leaves, Malacothrix is a twiggy, barren-looking plant, often overlooked on wildflower journeys.

## (211) Iris *(Iris sp.)*, ¾ A/S

**When:** The Iris on the opposite page was photographed in mid-June (April – July).

**Where:** The photo was taken on the Branscomb Road inland from the coast.

**What:** The subtle hue of the Iris will give you an idea of the incredible beauty and variety of colors they display. At least five species of Iris grow in Mendocino County.

## (212) Narrow Leaf Mule Ears *(Wyethia angustifolia)*, ¾ A/S

**When:** Narrow Leaf Mule Ears, one of the late-flowering members of the Aster family, bloom during early June (June – Aug.).

**Where:** Although *W. angustifolia* is found along the coast, it's more comfortable inland along the grassy road banks and wooded foothills of our inner valleys and coastal mountains. Mountain House Road and areas like Mt. Sanhedrin and Black Butte support fine specimens of Narrow Leaf Mule Ears.

**What:** A member of the Aster family, *W. angustifolia* is an attractive summer bloomer. Long, linear leaves set off the striking yellow of the ray flower petals. It's very satisfying that Narrow Leaf Mule Ears appear randomly along our dry summer road banks, calling out for more than a casual glance.

**(210) Malacothrix**

**(209) Seep-Willow**

**(211) Iris**

**(212) Narrow Leaf Mule Ears**

## (213) Phantom Orchid – Ghost Flower *(Cephalanthera austinae)*, ¾ A/S

**When:** Phantom Orchids start blooming by mid-June (June–July).

**Where:** Phantom Orchids grow sparingly, inland from the coast, in the shaded woodlands of mixed forests of redwood, fir, and oak. Also called Ghost Flowers, Phantom Orchids are found dispersed across the forest floor, colonizing in groups of ten or more. I recommend Admiral Wm. H. Standley State Recreation Area east of Branscomb as an excellent place to search for the lovely Ghost Flower.

**What:** A member of the Orchid family, *C. austinae* is said to reflect a ghostly appearance in the gloom of the deep forest. Ghost flowers reach heights of up to two feet. They have a delicate feathery quality, and when closely examined, their delicious scent of slightly burnt vanilla permeates the air.

## (214) Tiger Lily – Leopard Lily *(Lilium pardalinum)*, ½ A/S

**When:** You can expect to see our beautiful Tiger Lilies blooming in late June (June–July).

**Where:** *L. pardalinum* grows mostly west of Highway 101, always near water, in moist shaded woodlands. Tiger Lilies may be found on back roads that follow creeks and streams, such as Branscomb Road, Orr Springs Road, and Flynn Creek Road. My wife and I always look for *L. pardalinum* beyond Orr Hot Springs, along the headwaters of Big River.

**What:** A member of the Lily family, Tiger Lily, also called Leopard Lily, is one of our most colorful wildflowers, reaching heights of more than five feet. The many beautifully marked petals vary in color from orange to deep red, with as many as ten or more blossoms on one plant. I love to visit a secluded place located on a creek-side bank of Big River. I sit awhile and gaze at these remarkable creations, and can't help wondering what divine power produced such beauty.

## (215) Self-Heal *(Prunella vulgaris var. vulgaris)*, A/S +

**When:** Self-Heal appears in May, and reaches peak bloom in June (May–July).

**Where:** Self-Heal is found from the coastal headlands to the semi-shaded woods of the inner valley foothills. Some of the finest Self-Heal is found directly on the coast, with the Pt. Arena Lighthouse Road providing specimens outstanding in color and size.

**What:** A member of the Mint family, Self-Heal grows as a spike with purple-brown bracts and blue flowers. A native of Europe, Self-Heal was thought to have healing properties, particularly for diseases of the throat.

## (216) Redwood Lily – Chaparral Lily *(Lilium rubescens)*, ½ A/S

**When:** The remarkable beauty and fragrance of the Redwood Lily makes its presence known by mid-June (June–July).

**Where:** *L. rubescens* is found from the coastal plateaus inland, in open redwoods and woodlands, to the inner coastal mountain range, often in logged-over timberland. Most of the Redwood Lilies we find each year are located on the Branscomb Road to the coast, and on Orr Springs Road east of Comptche. Along the Avenue of the Giants, north of Myers Flat, we found one plant that was more than six feet tall and had nineteen blossoms.

**What:** A member of the Lily family, *L. rubescens* has beautiful white petals dotted with tiny purple spots. The petals turn a rich wine color as the plant ages. Redwood Lily is a glorious plant with a scent reminiscent of the finest perfume and the beauty of a true American native.

# JUNE

**(213) Phantom Orchid**

**(214) Tiger Lily**

**(215) Self-Heal**

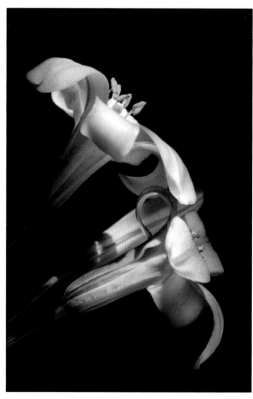

**(216) Redwood Lily**

## (217) Purple Milkweed *(Asclepias cordifolia)*, A/S

**When:** Expect to see Purple Milkweed blooming by mid-May at lower elevations (1,200 feet), and at higher elevations (4,000 feet) during July and August (May – Aug.).

**Where:** Purple Milkweed is found mostly at elevations above 1,200 feet, on the open and wooded slopes of our interior valleys and inner mountains. We find Asclepias growing along such back roads as Fish Rock Road, and inland to the east near Mt. Sanhedrin and Ham Pass north of Round Valley. A nice stand of Purple Milkweed grows on a grassy hillside slope just north of the Hopland Field Station.

**What:** *A. cordifolia* is a member of the Milkweed family. Purple Milkweed is an attractive plant showing loose clusters of purple flowers supported by a single smooth stem. The clean-looking opposite leaves are oval-shaped and a lovely shade of blue-green.

## (218) Chaparral Pea *(Pickeringia montana)*, A/S

**When:** The first flowers of the Chaparral Pea brighten our hillsides by late May or early June (June – Aug.).

**Where:** Although not common in our county, Chaparral Pea may be found on the coast on Old Highway 1 east of Gualala and on such back roads as Mountain View Road and the Old Toll Road. Inhabiting open and brushy slopes, *P. montana* is more prevalent in the Mayacamas Mountain range and east into Lake County.

**What:** A member of the Pea family *P. montana* is a large woody shrub that masses into large thickets. When in bloom, it adds superlative color to the dry chaparral-covered hillsides.

## (219) Showy Milkweed *(Asclepias speciosa)*, A/S +

**When:** Showy Milkweed starts to get showy between mid-May and June (June – July).

**Where:** *A. speciosa* likes the dry foothill slopes and woodlands of the inner mountains and valleys. Route 162 toward Mendocino Pass (through Round Valley and Covelo) provides excellent viewing of Showy Milkweed.

**What:** *A. speciosa* is a member of the Milkweed family. The flowers of Showy Milkweed are star-shaped, and curve somewhat like a tooth, forming ball-shaped clusters. When viewed closely, they'll make you wonder who was the architect.

## (220) Coyote Mint *(Monardella villosa ssp. villosa)*, A/S

**When:** Coyote Mint flowers toward mid-June, with the cycle of bloom lasting into August (June–August).

**Where:** *M. villosa* grows on the dry rocky slopes and chaparral-covered foothills of the interior valleys. It's always a pleasure to find Coyote Mint in bloom on Route 253 (Boonville – Ukiah) and the Old Toll Road east of Hopland.

**What:** Coyote Mint is a member of the Mint family. The flowers of *M. villosa* present beautiful hues of purple against the gray-browns of our dry rocky hillsides and canyon walls. Several other species of *Monardella* are found in the high country of the inner mountain range (see photograph #248, page 143 ).

# JUNE

**(217) Purple Milkweed**

**(218) Chaparral Pea**

**(219) Showy Milkweed**

**(220) Coyote Mint**

## (221) Brodiaea (Brodiaea elegans), A/S

**When:** You'll find *B. elegans* during the hot summer months of June and July (June–July).

**Where:** *Brodiaea elegans* is prevalent in the grassy meadows and hills of our interior valleys and along many of our back roads. The photograph on the opposite page was taken in an open meadow on Orr Springs Road.

**What:** *B. elegans* is a member of the Lily family.

## (222) Piperia – Habenaria (Piperia elongata), A/S+

**When:** Look for the elegant Piperia to flower in mid-June (June–Aug.).

**Where:** *P. elongata* ranges from the coast to the inner mountains, in shaded wooded slopes and hills, usually preferring elevations of 1,000 feet or higher. I look for Piperia on the Toll Road east of Hopland, and on the Branscomb–Laytonville Road.

**What:** A tall, slender plant up to two feet tall, *P. elongata* is a member of the Orchid family. Ascending a thin straight stem, each of the numerous, small, greenish-white flowers has a curved spur.

## (223) Harebell – California Bluebell (Campanula prenanthoides), 2 × A/S

**When:** Look for the small California Harebell to bloom by mid-June (June–July).

**Where:** Harebell may be found along the coast in mixed conifer forests, and in the foothills and mountains of the interior valleys. Wooded back roads and hillsides such as Orr Springs Road west of Comptche, and the upper trail in Low Gap County Park, provide quiet places to look for Bluebells.

**What:** A member of the Bellflower family, *C. prenanthoides* is a small, bell-shaped flower with a long, extended style. Although the plant may grow to a height of two feet, it's hard to see the small flowers in the shaded woods and forests where it resides.

## (224) Aralia – Elk Clover – California Spikenard (Aralia californica), 1/10 A/S

**When:** The large leaves and clustered flowers of California Spikenard will appear by early June (June–July).

**Where:** Aralia inhabits the moist stream banks and seeps, from the coastal redwoods to the inner mountain range. Areas with plentiful displays of Aralia are Elk Creek Basin, several miles south of the town of Elk on Highway 1, and Highway 128 inland from the coast, in the redwoods along the Navarro River.

**What:** *A. californica* is a member of the Ginseng family. Aralia may reach a height of more than eight feet. Its huge oval compound leaves may be more than a foot long, with the large stems supporting flower clusters the size and shape of golf balls.

# JUNE

**(221) Brodiaea**

**(222) Piperia**

**(223) Harebell**

**(224) Aralia**

## (225) Salmonberry Berry *(Rubus spectabilis)*, 2 × A/S

**When:** You can expect to see the lovely berries of *R. spectabilis* by late June (June–Aug.).

**Where:** Most of the coastal canyon creeks and streams running to the sea have fine displays of Salmon Berries; we particularly enjoy those at Russian Gulch and Van Damme State Parks. The day-use hiking trails afford easy access for viewing the lovely greenery and coastal plants that thrive in these miniature rainforests.

**What:** A member of the Rose family, *R. spectabilis* is a beautiful airy shrub that enhances any coastal setting. The lovely flower bloom of early spring, and the exotic salmon-colored berries that follow, give the Salmonberry shrub a special place in the order of things.

## (226) Thimbleberry *(Rubus parviflorus)*, A/S

**When:** The red berries of *R. parviflorus* brighten the coastal forests from mid-June to late August (June–Aug.).

**Where:** Thimbleberry shrub is found primarily in the redwood forests near or on the coast. To a lesser degree, it is also found inland in the mixed forests of the inner coastal mountain range. Van Damme State Park and Gualala River Road support fine specimens of Thimbleberry.

**What:** Thimbleberry belongs to the Rose family. Its bright-red berries add rich color to the coastal woods during the summer, and the sweet ripe berries are delicious.

## (227) Baneberry Berries – Red Baneberry *(Actaea rubra)*, A/S

**When:** The creamy-white flowers of Baneberry are apparent in the early spring; the beautiful red berries appear by late June (June–July).

**Where:** *A. rubra* is found mostly in the coastal forests along many of our back roads leading to the coast. The Branscomb Road and Van Damme State Park provide excellent viewing of these and other coastal plants.

**What:** Baneberry is a member of the Buttercup Family. The maple-like, narrow-toothed leaves support small white flowers in terminal clusters. Later in the summer months, the flowers turn to clusters of rich, shiny red berries. For all their beauty, it's important to know that all parts of the Baneberry plant are poisonous.

## (228) Twinberry *(Lonicera involucrata)*, A/S +

**When:** After the flowers bloom, shiny black berries will appear in June and last through August (June–Aug.).

**Where:** Twinberry is found in moist places on or near the coast, and less frequently inland in foothill woodlands near streams and seeps.

**What:** *L. involucrata* is a member of the Honeysuckle family. See photograph #165, page 99.

# JUNE

**(225) Salmon Berry**

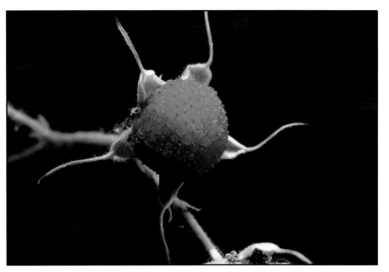

**(226) Thimbleberry**

**(227) Baneberry Berries**

**(228) Twinberry**

## (229) Coast Hedge Nettle – Chamisso's Hedge Nettle *(Stachys chamissonis)*, ¾ A/S

**When:** Coast Hedge Nettle appears by mid-June, with the bloom lasting into August (June–Aug.).

**Where:** You'll find Chamisso's Hedge Nettle in moist swamps and meadows close to the coast or directly on the coast. Very attractive stands of Coast Hedge Nettle thrive just north of Point Arena next to Highway 1, and farther north on Miner Hole Road.

**What:** A member of the Mint family, *S. chamissonis* wears a lovely shade of pink on its clusters of long-tubed flowers with scoop-like lower lips. The plant may reach a height of four feet, and, when grouped in large concentrations, puts on a marvelous show of color that adds much to the enjoyment of traveling along the coast.

## (230) Coastal Meadow Foam *(Limnanthes douglasii ssp. douglasii)*, A/S +

**When:** June is likely to be the prime month to find the coastal version of Meadow Foam (May–July).

**Where:** The photograph on the opposite page was taken on Pt. Arena Lighthouse Road. Other areas to explore are the coastal plains north of Point Arena, and the headlands of Manchester State Park.

**What:** *L. douglasii* is a member of the Meadow Foam family. I've included Meadow Foam again because the coastal version is a different subspecies from the Meadow Foam shown in photograph #19. The coastal version displays striking yellow petals with white tips—a very pleasing color combination.

## (231) Epilobium – Watson's Fireweed *(Epilobium ciliatum ssp. watsonii)*, 2 × A/S

**When:** You'll find *E. ciliatum* in bloom from late May through August (May–Aug.).

**Where:** Watson's Fireweed is found in wet seeps and moist grassy meadows immediately along the coast. My wife and I like to look for Watson's Fireweed and other flowers on Miner Hole Road north of Point Arena, and in a state preserve south of Westport.

**What:** A member of the Evening Primrose family, Epilobium is a coarse-looking plant with small pink flowers at the tips of stems up to three feet tall.

## (232) Pagoda Mint – Pennyroyal *(Mentha pulegium)*, A/S

**When:** Pagoda Mint blooms in early May and lasts well into September (May–Sept.).

**Where:** *M. pulegium* grows from the coast to the wooded foothills and meadows of the inner valleys. The photograph on the opposite page was taken in a coastal meadow south of Westport. Other special blooming areas are on Mountain House Road and Little Lake Valley north of Willits.

**What:** A member of the Mint family, Pennyroyal is an invasive non-native plant that can displace native species. I include it because it's already well established and it brightens many of our back roads. Large concentrations of Pagoda Mint will colonize in wet moist meadows and roadside ditches, making a great show of pink that lasts well into the dry season. Depending on where it grows, the color of Pagoda Mint varies from pink to purple.

**(229) Coast Hedge Nettle**

**(230) Coastal Meadow Foam**

**(231) Epilobium**

**(232) Pagoda Mint**

JULY

The endless summer days of the inland valleys drift by, the heat building and holding to the ground. The hills, burnt golden, mix with the flavors of wild Mint, Yampah, and Tarweed. To walk in the open fields and high grass hills is to carry the smells of summer on your clothes. The coastal headlands offer a new display of flowers and a cool refuge from the inland heat. The higher elevations of the inner mountain range have left the snow far behind, and it is time for the flowers of the high country to have their turn. The pitch-pine scent of the inland mountain forests, mixed with the searing heat of the day and the smell of campfires on cold nights; the burnt grass hills of mint and spice; and the cool salt air of the coastal plains, is all of Mendocino County and is unforgettable.

## (233) Jeffrey's Shooting Stars *(Dodecatheon jeffreyi)*, A/S +

**When:** In Mendocino County, Jeffrey's Shooting Stars bloom in June or early July, after the last snow has melted (June–July).

**Where:** *D. jeffreyi* is found above 5,000 feet, in wet meadows and seeps, and in open forests of the high mountains of the inner coastal range. During the early part of July, my wife and I have visited Plaskett Meadows, east of Mendocino Pass, and have enjoyed a grand colony of Shooting Stars. From a distance, they reflect and vibrate extraordinary colors ranging from shell pink to magenta, suggesting the work of a master impressionist.

**What:** High-mountain Shooting Stars are members of the Primrose family. *D. jeffreyi* is also found at higher elevations in the wet meadows and seeps of the mountains of the Pacific States.

## (234) Western Bistort – Lady's Thumb *(Polygonum bistortoides)*, A/S

**When:** Also called Lady's Thumb, Bistort blooms in early July (July–Aug.).

**Where:** Bistort blooms above 5,000 feet, in the wet meadows and seeps of the inner high mountains. You'll see small concentrations of Lady's Thumb scattered about such meadows near Black Butte and Mendocino Pass. To wander in the mountain meadows of our inner coastal range is to feel the energy of the high country, and delight in the flowers that inhabit these remarkable wild gardens.

**What:** The small white flowers of Lady's Thumb are clustered, forming an oval-shaped ball at the top of a one-to-two-foot leafless stem. Bistort is a member of the Buckwheat family.

## (235) Bog Orchid – Rein Orchid *(Platanthera leucostachys)*, A/S

**When:** Bog Orchid, also called Rein Orchid, (formerly in the genus *Habenaria*) begins blooming in late June or early July (July–Aug.).

**Where:** The white Rein Orchid grows sparsely along the coast, but is more abundant above 4,000 feet, in the wet meadows and streams of our inner mountains . We always find white Bog Orchids in the moist meadows and forest openings near Mendocino Pass and Black Butte.

**What:** *P. leucostachys* is a member of the Orchid family. Bog Orchids reach a height of three feet, with numerous pure white blossoms growing on a spike-like stem, each flower having a long, curved spur.

## (236) Large Leaf Lupine *(Lupinus polyphyllus var. polyphyllus)*, ¾ A/S

**When:** Look for *L. polyphyllus* blooming at the higher elevations in early July (June–Aug.).

**Where:** Large Leaf Lupine is found in coastal marshes and strands, and inland at the upper elevations of the inner coastal mountains. The photograph on the opposite page was taken in a moist meadow next to a clear-running stream near Mendocino Pass.

**What:** A member of the Pea family, *L. polyphyllus* may reach a height of more than four feet. With its large, bright-green leaflets and numerous spikes of purplish blue flowers, it has the look of the tropics. This handsome plant adds charm and beauty to the landscape wherever it's found.

**(233) Jeffrey's Shooting Stars**

**(234) Western Bistort**

**(235) Bog Orchid**

**(236) Large Leaf Lupine**

## (237) Steershead *(Dicentra uniflora), 3 × A/S*

**When:** Steershead appears in our high mountains when the ground is exposed after the last snow has melted. Because of the difficulty in predicting snow levels in late spring, the blooming time varies from May to early July (May–July).

**Where:** Rare in our county, *D. uniflora* is found only at elevations above 5,000 feet, in the inner mountains near Mendocino Pass. Search for Steershead below the summit of Black Butte in wet, gravelly flats in the openings of mixed pine and fir, and near melting snow banks above Wells Cabin Campground east of Anthony Peak. The photograph of Steershead on the opposite page was taken in Lassen Volcanic Park, and is approximately three times the actual size of the flower. Because of its small size, you'll have to look closely to find this unique plant.

**What:** *D. uniflora* is a member of the Poppy family. The small pink flowers are perfect miniatures of a steer's head. These fascinating flowers are common to the northern Sierra Nevada, through the Pacific States, and into British Columbia.

## (238) Skyrocket Gilia *(Ipomopsis aggregata ssp. formosissima)*, A/S

**When:** Skyrocket Gilia, also called Scarlet Gilia, is a high-mountain wildflower; look for it to bloom in July (July–Aug.).

**Where:** Rare in Mendocino County, *I. aggregata* is found only in our high mountains east of Covelo, near the summit of Mendocino pass. One area to search for Scarlet Gilia is on the open rocky slopes and woods around Black Butte.

**What:** *I. aggregata* is a member of the Phlox family. The brilliant scarlet color and trumpet-shaped flowers of Scarlet Gilia make this plant easily identified and delightful to find. Skyrocket Gilia may reach a height of more than two feet, on stems that are sticky to the touch and have as many as eight to ten flowers forming loose clusters.

## (239) Pinedrops *(Pterospora andromedea)*, A/S

**When:** You'll see the first Pinedrops by mid-July (July–Aug.).

**Where:** Pinedrops grow above 5,000 feet, in the pine and fir forests of the inner mountain range. The semi-open woods near Mendocino Pass provide a suitable environment for Pinedrops to flourish.

**What:** *P. andromedea* is a member of the Heath family. Pinedrops may reach a height of more than two feet, mostly before the reddish, urn-shaped flowers have had a chance to open. *P. andromedea* is a saprophyte, receiving its nourishment from the dead and decaying organic matter found on the forest floor.

## (240) Showy Phlox *(Phlox speciosa var. occidentalis)*, A/S +

**When:** The colorful Showy Phlox blooms by late June or early July (June–Aug.).

**Where:** *P. speciosa* is found in the wooded openings of mixed pine and fir above 4,000 feet, on the northeastern boundary of our inner mountain range.

**What:** Showy Phlox is a beautiful member of the Phlox family. Its five petals are a lovely shade of pink, bilobed and marked with white toward the center. Seeing Showy Phlox in full color for the first time in a forest opening will warm your soul and bring a smile to your face.

# JULY

**(237) Steershead**

**(238) Skyrocket Gilia**

**(239) Pinedrops**

**(240) Showy Phlox**

## (241) Gray Mule Ears *(Wyethia helenioides)*, ¾ A / S

**When:** Gray Mule Ears usually bloom in early July (June–Aug.).

**Where:** Although *W. helenioides* is found in the foothills and woodlands of the inner valleys, perhaps the most spectacular show of blossoms is along Route 162, on the mountain slopes and meadows leading to Mendocino Pass.

**What:** A member of the Aster family, Gray Mule Ears are aptly named because of their color and shape. The beautiful silvery gray color of the leaves, which resemble the ears of a mule, frames the yellow ray flowers, adding a unique color display to the hills during the early summer months. Along with the flower display there is a distinctive scent—very aromatic, pungent, and deeply satisfying.

## (242) Prince's Pine *(Chimaphila menziesii)*, A / S +

**When:** The time to look for Prince's Pine, also called Pipsissewa, is July (July–Aug.).

**Where:** *C. menziesii* is a woodland plant found in redwood, pine, and fir forests. Prince's Pine grows in woodlands near the coast in the area of Orr Springs Road, and inland in the pine forests of Mt. Sanhedrin and Mendocino Pass.

**What:** Interesting in flower shape and design, *C. menziesii* is a member of the Heath family. The waxy, pink, crown-shaped flowers are clustered on the top of a six-to-ten-inch stem, with linear leaves showing small, sharp teeth.

## (243) Azure Penstemon *(Penstemon azureus var. azureus)*, A / S +

**When:** Because Azure Penstemon is found at higher elevations, you can expect to find this lovely species blooming from early June to late August.

**Where:** Azure Penstemon is more common to the inner coastal mountains, in dry chaparral and open wooded areas of mixed pine and fir. Mendocino Pass, Anthony Peak, and Leech Lake Mountain Road all support fine specimens of *P. azureus*.

**What:** A member of the Figwort family, Azure Penstemon is one at least ten species of Penstemon found in Mendocino County.

## (244) Mountain Sidalcea *(Sidalcea oregana ssp. hydrophila)*, A / S +

**When:** Mountain Sidalcea will bloom in the high country from late June through July (June-Aug.).

**Where:** *S. oregana* is rare in Mendocino County, and is found only in the higher elevations of the inner mountain range. The photograph of Sidalcea on the opposite page was taken near the summit of Anthony Peak. A narrow dirt road that turns north off route 162 at Mendocino Pass will lead you to Wells Cabin Campground and the summit. While driving that road, my wife and I spotted the jewel-like Mountain Sidalcea. Several plants were located near a seep-spring, sharing space with a patch of Corn Lilies and Cinquefoil. I was able to photograph this lovely plant against a shadow, creating the black background you see in the photo.

**What:** *S. Oregana* is a member of the Mallow family. Mendocino County contains at least ten species of Sidalcea that range from the coast (see photograph #169, page 101) to the inner mountains. All are beautiful.

**(241) Gray Mule Ears**

**(242) Prince's Pine**

**(243) Azure Penstemon**

**(244) Mountain Sidalcea**

## (245) Sierra Onion *(Allium campanulatum)*, A/S

**When:** *A. campanulatum* blooms in late June or early July (June–July).

**Where:** Sierra Onion is found at elevations above 5,000 feet, on gravel flats and in the open woods of the inner coastal mountain range. The photograph on the opposite page was taken on a rocky slope near the summit of Anthony Peak. I love looking for the beautiful Sierra Onion and the other wildflowers that thrive around Black Butte and Anthony Peak. There will always be something special for me about the remoteness and beauty of the high country and the rare flowers that grace these wild and lonely places.

**What:** *A. campanulatum* is a member of the Lily family. At least a dozen species of Allium grow in Mendocino County, among them the Sierra Onion, considered by many the most beautiful in appearance and color.

## (246) Mountain Buckwheat *(Eriogonum compositum var. compositum)*, A/S

**When:** Look for this mountain flower to bloom by late June or early July (July–Aug.).

**Where:** *E. compositum* is found in the rocky cliffs and flats near or on the summits of our inner high mountains. The photograph of *E. compositum* on the opposite page was taken close to the summit of Anthony Peak.

**What:** The flowers of Mountain Buckwheat are sulfur yellow, and grow on stems up to two feet tall. The lower leaves are densely hairy and whitish, with the upper leaves smooth and green. The remarkable sulfur color of this robust member of the Buckwheat family is startling when seen against the rocky cliffs and ledges where it grows.

## (247) Mountain Spring Beauty *(Cardamine californica)*, A/S

**When:** Mountain Spring Beauty is found blooming in the inner mountain range in late June or early July, after the snow has melted (July–Aug.).

**Where:** You'll find this species of Cardamine in the moist forests and open meadows of our inner coastal mountains.

**What:** Mountain Spring Beauty is a member of the Mustard family.

## (248) Mountain Monardella *(Monardella odoratissima ssp. glauca)*, A/S

**When:** You can expect to see Mountain Monardella blooming by late June or early July (July–Aug.).

**Where:** Rare in Mendocino County, *M. odoratissima* is found only in the higher elevations of the inner coastal mountain range. The photograph I took on the opposite page was on the summit of Anthony Peak. From a distance, the flowers of the shrub-like plant appeared to be levitating. Drawing closer, I noticed hundreds of small orange butterflies hovering around the blossoms, landing when there was room, all dining frenziedly on a sumptuous nectar feast.

**What:** Mountain Monardella is a member of the Mint family. We have several species of Monardella that are very similar in appearance. The one called Coyote Mint, shown in photograph #220, is more commonly found in the woodland foothills and rocky slopes at lower elevations. All of the Monardella are woody in appearance, and grow in shrub-like clumps up to a foot or more in height.

**(245) Sierra Onion**

**(246) Mountain Buckwheat**

**(247) Mountain Spring Beauty**

**(248) Mountain Monardella**

## (249) Cinquefoil *(Potentilla glandulosa ssp. ashlandica)*, A/S +

**When:** Cinquefoil grows in many habitats and varied elevations in Mendocino County. The blooming cycle of the genus *Potentilla* occurs from May through August (May – Aug.).

**Where:** Several species of Cinquefoil grow in Mendocino County, on coastal headlands, inland in foothill woodlands, and on the high mountains of our inner coastal range. I took the photograph of *P. glandulosa* on the opposite page on a beautiful July day in a high mountain meadow near Mendocino Pass.

**What:** A member of the Rose family, Cinquefoil is common to our county and the Pacific States. Cinquefoil grows to a height of more than two feet, its lovely creamy-yellow flowers branching from a single main stem. The delicate appearance of Cinquefoil in a high meadow on a summer's day will give you reason to stop and linger awhile.

## (250) Pussy Paws *(Calyptridium umbellatum)*, A/S

**When:** Pussy paws usually bloom from late June through August (June – Aug.).

**Where:** You'll find Pussy Paws above 4,000 feet in the high mountains of our inner coastal range, growing in meadows, on gravel flats, and in open forests. The photograph of Pussy Paws on the opposite page was taken in one of Nature's splendid meadows near Mendocino Pass.

**What:** *C. umbellatum* is a member of the Purslane family. Pussy Paws are a delight to find. Their dark green leaves lie in flat clusters scattered about on the gravelly ground. The tightly bunched pink blossoms radiate out into bouquets of flowers that look just like the pussycat paws they're named for.

## (251) Spreading Phlox *(Phlox sp.)*, A/S

**When:** Several species of Phlox grow in Mendocino County. Spreading Phlox blooms in late June or early July (July – Aug.).

**Where:** The photograph on the opposite page was taken above 5,000 feet in the inner mountain range near the summit of Anthony Peak.

**What:** A member of the Phlox Family, Spreading Phlox forms colorful mats that carpet openings in the forest floor, grassy meadows, and rock-strewn hillsides.

## (252) Meadow Penstemon – *(Penstemon rydbergii var. oreocharis)*, A/S

**When:** Meadow Penstemon blooms in late June or early July (June – Aug.).

**Where:** *P. rydbergii* may be found in the moist high mountain meadows and open forests of the inner coastal range. Large concentrations of Meadow Penstemon grow near Mendocino Pass on Route 162 east of Covelo.

**What:** A member of the Figwort family, *P. rydbergii* is one of at least ten species of Penstemon found in our county. The flowers are whorled around a six-to-ten-inch stem, and when growing in large masses, produce a sea of deep blue-purple that undulates in the slightest mountain breeze.

**(249) Cinquefoil**

**(250) Pussy Paws**

**(251) Spreading Phlox**

**(252) Meadow Penstemon**

## (253) Corn Lily *(Veratrum californicum)*, ¹⁄₁₀ A / S

**When:** Corn Lilies begin to bloom by late June or early July (June–Aug.).

**Where:** Although Corn Lilies may be found on the coast and inland to the inner mountains, I always think of *V. californicum* as a high-mountain wildflower. Corn Lilies seek out moist seeps and meadows, and are most likely to live in the inner mountains near Mendocino Pass and Mt. Sanhedrin. The photograph on the opposite page was taken on Route 162 leading to Mendocino Pass, in a moist meadow above 4,000 feet.

**What:** *V. Californicum* is a member of the Lily family. Corn Lilies may grow five feet tall, with large, parallel, veined leaves supporting loose, irregularly branched clusters of white star-shaped flowers. A California native, *V. californicum* lives throughout the state's high mountains.

## (254) Blazing Star *(Mentzelia laevicaulis)*, ½ A / S

**When:** Blazing Stars have a long flowering cycle; the length depending on where they grow. The most consistent time to find *M. laevicaulis* in full bloom is the third week in July (July–Oct.).

**Where:** Although somewhat rare in Mendocino County, Blazing Stars may be found in several locations, including the gravelly washes of the Eel and Russian Rivers. We always find a number of plants on a gravelly bank of Pieta Creek where it empties into the Russian River, and on a dry hillside bank next to the Eel, just south of Dos Rios. Round Valley has several fine specimens on the northeast end of the valley, in a gravel wash near Small Creek.

**What:** A member of the Loasa family, the flower of *M. laevicaulis* has superb coloring: the beautifully shaped blossoms are pale yellow, with as many as seven or eight flowers growing from coarse-looking branches, and a main stem that ranges in height up to four feet. The photograph on the opposite page was taken at sunrise in October 1992 along a dry wash near Lake Pillsbury. The early-morning light ignited the flower into a starburst of soft yellow. I was able to position my camera so the flower was in the foreground and the shadow of a low bridge in the background, causing the background in the print to go black.

## (255) Western Blue Flag *(Iris missouriensis)*, ½ A / S

**When:** Western Blue Flag begins blooming in late June or early July (July–Aug.).

**Where:** Blue Flag is found in meadows and side hills above 4,000 feet, in the inner mountains of the coastal range east of Covelo on Route 162.

**What:** Blue Flag is a member of the Iris family and is one of several species common to our county. While hiking in a mountain meadow near Black Butte, I came upon a large colony of Blue Flags that were nearly three feet tall and tightly clustered as if planted by human hands. I sat for a time in the gentle wind and sun, unwilling to leave Nature's enchanting handiwork.

## (256) Bitter Dogbane *(Apocynum androsaemifolium)*, A / S

**When:** Bitter Dogbane, sometimes called Spreading Dogbane, blooms in late June or early July (July–Aug.).

**Where:** Though occasionally found in the redwoods and foothill woodlands, Spreading Dogbane is more common to the higher elevations of the inner coastal mountains.

**What:** *A. androsaemifolium* is a member of the Dogbane family. The small, pink, bell-shaped flowers are hard to miss on the open mountain slopes.

**(253) Corn Lily**

**(254) Blazing Star**

**(255) Western Blue Flag**

**(256) Bitter Dogbane**

## (257) Horsemint (Agastache urticifolia), A/S

**When:** Horsemint is a summer bloomer; look for it at the end of June or early July (July – Aug.)

**Where:** Horsemint grows inland in colonies near creeks, streams, and moist seeps. It is selective in choosing where to live. The Russian River near Ukiah, and Outlet Creek near Longvale, provide the right habitat for Horsemint to flourish. I located several beautiful specimens of *A. urticifolia* in a moist seep alongside Route 162 leading to Mendocino Pass.

**What:** A member of the Mint family, *A. urticifolia* has a lovely feathery quality, with pink-to-white flowers in terminal brush-like clusters. Horsemint reaches a height of five feet, and when found in large colonies presents a charming color display on a hot July afternoon.

## (258) Pearly Everlasting (Anaphalis margaritacea), A/S

**When:** We see the first bloom of Pearly Everlasting in late June or early July. On the coast the bloom cycle lasts well into September (June – Sept.).

**Where:** Pearly Everlasting grows abundantly along the coastal headlands and in the wooded foothills of the inland valleys. You'll find *A. margaritacea* on the banks of our back roads leading too the coast. The north end of Manchester Beach State Park, in the Alder Creek area, is a wildflower paradise and a perfect place to look for Pearly Everlasting and other coastal plants.

**What:** *A. margaritacea* is a member of the Aster family. The common name, Pearly Everlasting, suits this wildflower well, for it seems to bloom forever.

## (259) Narrow Leaf Milkweed (Asclepias fascicularis), A/S

**When:** The early Narrow Leaf Milkweed blooms at the end of June or the first part of July (June – Aug.).

**Where:** *A. fascicularis* is found on dry grassy road banks, wooded foothills, and on the slopes of the inner coastal mountain range. You'll find Narrow Leaf Milkweed on such back roads as Mountain House Road, Orr Springs Road, and Route 162 east of Round Valley.

**What:** *A. fascicularis* is a member of the Milkweed family. The small, purple-tinted flowers are congested into umbrella-like clusters at the end of stems more than two feet tall. The long, narrow leaves are arranged in whorls, giving *A. fascicularis* a light, airy quality that's outstanding in the hot summer landscape.

## (260) Tarweed (Hemizonia congesta ssp. luzulifolia), 1½ × A/S

**When:** Tarweed, liking hot weather, starts blooming in early July (July – Sept.).

**Where:** Although not common to Mendocino County, *H. congesta* is found on the dry, open slopes and wooded foothills of the interior valleys. Low Gap County Park and Orr Springs Road both support large concentrations of Tarweed.

**What:** A member of the Aster family, *H. congesta* has a pungent, balsamic aroma that is quite pleasing to the nose. After hiking the high hills and meadows, the fragrance of Tarweed on my boots and clothes forever reminds me of Mendocino County on a summer's day.

**(257) Horsemint**

**(258) Pearly Everlasting**

**(259) Narrow Leaf Milkweed**

**(260) Tarweed**

## (261) Centaury *(Centaurium muehlenbergii)*, A/S

**When:** Centaury flowers begin brightening the countryside by early July. The cycle of bloom lasts into early September (July – Sept.).

**Where:** Centaury is found from the coast to the inner mountains, preferring moist areas. The coastal habitats to explore for Centaury include Greenwood Creek below the small town of Elk, and Big River next to Mendocino Village. Inland from the coast you'll see impressive displays of Centaury on grassy hillsides and meadows, usually where the slope of the hill collects small amounts of moisture. Roads similar to Mountain House Road provide excellent samples of Centaury.

**What:** A member of the Gentian family, *C. muehlenbergii* is robust and colorful, and will surprise and thrill you when you see it on a hot day in July or August.

## (262) Moth Mullein *(Verbascum blatteria)*, A/S

**When:** Moth Mullein has a long blooming season, and is seen flowering from June to October (June – Oct.).

**Where:** *V. blatteria* is quite common, and may be found along many of Mendocino County's back roads. Eastside Road and Mountain House Road provide quiet places to observe the Moth Mullein and other wildflowers.

**What:** A member of the Figwort family, Moth Mullein is naturalized from Eurasia. The woolly reddish-brown center (resembling a small moth) and the bright lemon hue of the petals make the Moth Mullein an interesting stop on your wildflower journey.

## (263) Verbena – Western Verbena *(Verbena lasiostachys var. lasiostachys)*, A/S

**When:** One of several verbenas, *V. lasiostachys* blooms at the end of June or in early July (July – Sept.).

**Where:** *V. lasiostachys* is not as common as some other Verbenas, but you'll find it in the higher elevations and foothills of the inner coastal mountain range. The photograph on the opposite page was taken at an elevation of 3,000 feet on Route 162 leading to Mendocino Pass.

**What:** *V. lasiostachys* is a member of the Vervain family. Western Verbena shows clusters of blue or pink blossoms growing on a number of long, slender, spike-like stems. A native plant, Western Verbena may be found from Baja to Oregon.

## (264) Chicory *(Cichorium intybus)*, A/S

**When:** In early July, Chicory flowers seem to appear overnight, suddenly filling the roadsides with color (June – Sept.).

**Where:** Chicory grows throughout Mendocino County, with perhaps the most conspicuous displays in the fields and meadows of Round Valley, along the road banks of Highway 101, and on such back roads as Mountain House Road.

**What:** A native of England, Chicory is a member of the Aster family. The fleshy root of Chicory has long been dried, ground, and then roasted to make a substitute for, or an enhancement of, coffee. Chicory's startling blue color is always a surprise when you see it still blooming in early October.

**(261) Centaury**

**(262) Moth Mullein**

**(263) Verbena**

**(264) Chicory**

## (265) Wild Buckwheat *(Eriogonum sp.)*, A/S

**When:** The many species of *Eriogonum sp.* start blooming in early July (June – Sept.).

**Where:** Common to many different habitats, Wild Buckwheat is likely to be found on coastal plateaus and strands, and along many of our inland back roads, and on rocky hillsides and slopes all the way to the inner coastal mountains.

**What:** *Eriogonum sp.* is a member of the Buckwheat family. We have a number of buckwheat species in our county, differing in color and size. The flower heads are quite colorful and attractive, both when first in bloom and again as they age. The small intricate flowers of Buckwheat, shown in the photograph on the opposite page, can be better appreciated when closely examined in the field.

## (266) Queen Anne's Lace – Wild Carrot *(Daucus carota)*, A/S +

**When:** Queen Anne's Lace blooms from May to late October (May – Oct.).

**Where:** *D. carota* may be found throughout Mendocino County. Large masses of wild carrot bloom along the sides of many of our roads, such as Highway 128 in Anderson Valley, and Highway 1 on the coast.

**What:** A native of Asia and Europe, Queen Anne's Lace is a member of the Carrot family.

## (267) Teasel *(Dipsacus sativus)*, A/S

**When:** Teasel plants start their bloom in July, the new blossoms mixing among the dried plants from the previous year (July – Aug.).

**Where:** Teasel forms dense thickets along many of our county roads. Taking a closer look when the Teasel cone is in bloom, you'll find tiny blossoms formed into bands of pink.

**What:** A member of the Teasel family, *Dipsacus* migrated from Eurasia. I include Teasel in this book because I like the way it looks, and because it makes great decorations when aged and dry.

## (268) Yellow Calycadenia *(Calycadenia truncata)*, 1½ × A/S

**When:** Somewhat rare in Mendocino County, *C. truncata* blooms toward the latter part of July (July – Sept.).

**Where:** We have several species of Calycadenia in the county. *C. truncata* is the one you'll find in Low Gap County Park. The effect of this patch of yellow on a dry slope in July and early August is outstanding.

**What:** Yellow Calycadenia is a member of the Aster family. The species that grows in Low Gap County Park forms a large colony on rocky soil. It shows as many as nine or ten small flowers grouped on a single branched stem. The rich shade of yellow of Calycadenia flowers is simply superb against the open hillsides. The August heat does nothing to discourage this lovely plant.

**(265) Wild Buckwheat**

**(266) Queen Anne's Lace**

**(267) Teasel**

**(268) Yellow Calycadenia**

## (269) Stick Flower *(Stephanomeria virgata)*, 2 × A / S

**When:** Stick flower blooms from July through September (July–Sept.).

**Where:** Although not common in our county, *S. virgata* may be found growing in thin rocky soil on road banks and hillsides inland from the coast. I find it along the rocky hillsides of such roads as Low Gap Road and Orr Springs Road.

**What:** A member of the Aster family, Stick Flower is leafless and twiggy, and thrives in hot dry conditions. The flowers are widely scattered on branched woody stems that grow to three feet in height. Although Stick Flower, with its meager bloom, doesn't draw your immediate attention, it does capture the essence of the dry and unbearably hot hillsides of summer.

## (270) Straw Flower *(Gnaphalium californicum)*, A / S

**When:** The white flower buds of *G. californicum* emerge in July, and then seem to stay closed forever, until at last they open in August (July–Oct.).

**Where:** Straw Flower is not common in Mendocino County, but it may be found in widely scattered areas. It grows in patches of two or three plants on side hills and the banks of back roads such as Mountain House Road, Orr Springs Road, and Fish Rock Road.

**What:** A member of the Aster family, Straw Flower, with its many-branched stems, reaches a height of more than three feet. The straw-like color and texture of the flowers is worth a close look, and while you gaze, the fragrance of the flower will remind you of fresh-cut celery.

## (271) Sweet Fennel *(Foeniculum vulgare)*, ½ A / S

**When:** You'll see Sweet Fennel in bloom by late June or early July (July–Oct.).

**Where:** Fennel is found from the coast to the inner valleys and foothills of the inner mountains. Fennel loves the grassy banks and meadows along the sides of many of our back roads, such as Mountain House Road and Eastside Road.

**What:** A member of the Carrot family, Sweet Fennel arrived here from the Mediterranean. Though not native to America, it deserves a place in this book. The plant has the distinctive aroma of anise, and all parts of it may be eaten—it's delicious in salads and vegetable dishes.

## (272) Yampah *(Perideridia kelloggii)*, A / S +

**When:** Yampah is a late bloomer, so you'll see the first flowers by mid-July or early August (July–Sept.).

**Where:** Although found from the coast to the inner coastal mountains, Yampah loves the hot, dry hillsides of our inner valleys. You'll find dense patches of *P. kelloggii* along the sides of Mountain House Road and Orr Springs Road.

**What:** *P. Kelloggii* is a member of the Carrot family. To enjoy Yampah and the other flowers of summer, sit quietly near a country road on a July afternoon, and feel the heat embracing the fields and meadows and holding all things still; become aware of the scent of dry grass and wildflowers drifting slowly on the shimmering air.

**(269) Stick Flower**

**(270) Straw Flower**

**(271) Sweet Fennel**

**(272) Yampah**

## (273) Sundew *(Drosera rotundifolia)*, A/S

**When:** The Sundew's leaves are in place most of the year; the tiny white flowers start blooming around mid-June or early July (July–Sept.).

**Where:** In Mendocino County, *D. rotundifolia* is primarily a coastal plant. Sundew is found in sphagnum bogs that dot the headlands and meadows on or near the coast. I haven't yet seen *D. rotundifolia* in Mendocino County—the photograph on the opposite page was taken in Lassen Volcanic National Park.

**What:** Sundew is an insectivorous plant, that is, it feeds on small insects. The many leaf blades have red-stalked hairs, the surface of the blades and hairs covered with a glutinous substance. Insects attracted to the Sundew become trapped by the sticky leaf blades and, unable to escape, are digested for their nitrogen content. The tiny white flowers sit atop a thin stem no more than eight inches tall, with the leaf blades lying close to the ground. *D. rotundifolia* is a member of the Sundew family.

## (274) Coastal Lotus *(Lotus corniculatus)*, 2 × A/S

**When:** Yellow Coastal Lotus blooms from early June through September (June–Sept.).

**Where:** *L. corniculatus* forms dense masses of floral color on coastal meadows and headlands, and is one of the few flowers still blooming in late September. It is also found inland in abundance.

**What:** A native of Europe, Coastal Lotus is a member of the Pea family. I include *L. corniculatus* because of the striking yellow color it provides during much of the summer and fall.

## (275) Coastal Buckwheat *(Eriogonum latifolium)*, A/S

**When:** The handsome flower display of Coastal Buckwheat appears in early June (June–Aug.).

**Where:** *E. latifolium* grows directly on the coast, finding room to spread and flourish on coastal meadows, headlands, and cliffs. The headlands along the Haul Road north of Fort Bragg provide a remarkable display of Coastal Buckwheat.

**What:** A member of the Buckwheat family, *E. latifolium* is an attractive open plant. Its deep pink flower heads are large, round, and tightly clustered. The oblong leaves cluster at the base of the plant, forming large mats of silvery gray, in perfect contrast to the lovely hue of the flowers.

## (276) Purple Ruffles *(Orobanche californica ssp. californica)*, A/S

**When:** The early bloom of Purple Ruffles occurs in late June, with the peak bloom arriving the first week of July (July–Aug.).

**Where:** Although I have never found *O. californica* in quantity, you'll see it growing along the coast on the headlands and stable dunes. Purple Ruffles may be found along the road into the Pt. Arena lighthouse, and on the headlands north of Pudding Creek.

**What:** *O. californica* is a member of the Broomrape family. Purple Ruffles is a parasitic leafless plant that attaches itself to the roots of the coastal Gumplant. When searching for Purple Ruffles along the coastal headlands, check the leaves around and underneath the many patches of Yellow Gumplant (see photo #277, page 159).

**(273) Sundew**

**(274) Coastal Lotus**

**(275) Coastal Buckwheat**

**(276) Purple Ruffles**

## (277) Gumplant – Grindelia *(Grindelia stricta var. stricata)*, A/S

**When:** Coastal Gumplant flowers by early June, but count on July as the month when Grindelia reaches peak bloom (June–Sept.).

**Where:** Grindelia thrives on the coastal headlands, sea bluffs, and dunes from Gualala in the south to the Sinkyone Wilderness in the north. Nearly all the bluffs show fine displays of common Grindelia. Two areas offering excellent Gumplant viewing are the headlands north of Pudding Creek, and the Jefferson Way headlands south of Fort Bragg.

**What:** A member of the Aster family, *G. stricta* lies prostrate or semi-erect, and exudes a clear, sticky substance beneath the flower heads next to the stem. Grindelia colonizes into small groups on the ocean bluffs, creating a lovely yellow hue that complements and pays homage to the other coastal flowers.

## (278) Ladies' Tresses *(Spiranthes romanzoffiana)*, A/S +

**When:** You'll notice the first Ladies' Tresses blooming by the first week in July (July–Aug.).

**Where:** My wife and I look for Ladies' Tresses on or near the coast in wet bogs and meadows. We also look several miles inland, in the stunted undergrowth of huckleberry and juniper on such roads as Caspar–Little Lake. Ladies' Tresses may also be found inland, in the wet meadows of northern Little Lake Valley north of Willits.

**What:** A member of the Orchid family, Ladies' Tresses grow as spikes, with numerous small white flowers forming a tight spiral on a single stem up to eighteen inches tall. The intricate design of Ladies' Tresses is evident in the photograph on the opposite page. The image was taken on the Caspar–Little Lake Road in late July.

## (279) Coastal Piperia *(Piperia elegans)*, A/S

**When:** Look for the stout spikes of *P. elegans* to bloom in early July (July–Aug.).

**Where:** Coastal Piperia is found on the coastal headlands and bluffs from Gualala to Westport. Although Coastal Piperia is not common, I suggest exploring the headlands at the north end of Manchester Beach State Park as a likely area for viewing it.

**What:** *Piperia elegans* is a member of the Orchid family. Coastal Piperia grows up to twelve inches tall on a stout, cone-shaped spike of numerous small white flowers. I find *P. elegans* an unusually attractive sight growing on the windswept coastal bluffs, its delicate flowers sturdy enough to withstand the near-constant wind sweeping in from the sea.

## (280) Gentian – Prairie Gentian *(Gentiana affinis var. ovata)*, A/S

**When:** The beautiful blue color of *Gentiana affinis* becomes noticeable by early July (July–Aug.).

**Where:** *Gentiana affinis* is found directly on the coastal headlands and meadows, and inland in the barrens east of Mendocino Village and the City of Fort Bragg. Quiet areas to search for Prairie Gentian are on the Caspar–Little Lake Road and the Jefferson Way headlands south of Fort Bragg.

**What:** *Gentiana affinis* is a member of the Gentian family, and is one of several species that grow in Mendocino County. The Gentian flower holds a special place in the plant kingdom; its lovely blue color and vase-like shape are always a treat to find.

**(277) Gumplant**

**(278) Ladies' Tresses**

**(279) Coastal Piperia**

**(280) Gentian**

## (281) Fireweed *(Epilobium angustifolium ssp. circumvagum)*, ½ A/S

**When:** Look for Fireweed, also called Willow Herb, to bloom in early July; the cycle of bloom lasts into late August (July–Aug.).

**Where:** In Mendocino County, Fireweed grows primarily on the coast, but is occasionally found inland in scattered locations east of Highway 101. We find Willow Herb on the coast in several places, including a shrub-covered bank above eye level along Highway 1 south of Elk Creek Basin, and along Highway 1 a few miles north of Cleone.

**What:** Native to America and Europe, Willow Herb is found in abundance in the mountains of North America, particularly where fire has swept through. A member of the Evening Primrose family, the bright-pink-to-red flowers of Fireweed are in long terminal spikes. Striking in size as well as color, the Willow Herb found along our coast reaches heights of more than six feet. Native Americans and many Europeans enjoyed Fireweed as a source of food, finding the young shoots and stems pleasing in soups, and the leaves good in salads.

## (282) Brownie Thistle *(Cirsium quercetorum)*, A/S

**When:** The blooming cycle of Brownie Thistle begins in late June or early July (July–August).

**Where:** *Cirsium quercetorum* grows only along coastal bluffs and headlands. One of our favorite locations for finding Brownie Thistle and other coastal wildflowers is on the headlands along the Haul Road north of Fort Bragg. Several trails wind their way along the bluffs, allowing for leisurely walking and pleasurable wildflower viewing.

**What:** A member of the Aster family, *C. quercetorum*, with its creamy-brown color and thistle-like appearance, is accurately described by its common name, Brownie Thistle. *C. quercetorum* grows in scattered clumps close to the ground, with no evidence of a stem. It adds unique color and texture to the coastal headlands.

## (283) Sneezeweed *(Helenium bolanderi)*, A/S +

**When:** The handsome flowers of Sneezeweed appear in late June or early July (July–Sept.).

**Where:** Sneezeweed is found along the coast in the moist meadows and swamps of our headlands and bluffs. I look for it in the Jefferson Way headlands south of Fort Bragg; I counted more than 100 plants blooming near a bog in this location. A similar but different species of Sneezeweed grows in the forests of our inner coastal mountains.

**What:** *Helenium bolanderi*, a member of the Aster family, grows taller than two feet. With its brown, globe-shaped head and many brilliant yellow ray petals, Sneezeweed is an unforgettable sight when viewed in mass on a summer day.

## (284) Angelica *(Angelica hendersonii)*, ¼ A/S

**When:** Angelica blooms in July, its flowering cycle lasting into September (July–Sept.).

**Where:** Angelica grows on the immediate coast, on coastal headlands, meadows, and ocean bluffs. Large concentrations of Angelica thrive on the coastal plateaus along the Haul Road north of Pudding Creek.

**What:** A member of the Carrot family, Angelica is a stout-looking plant that grows taller than two feet. As Angelica ages, its ball-shaped flowers turn from white to a lovely rust-like magenta.

**(281) Fireweed**

**(282) Brownie Thistle**

**(283) Sneezeweed**

**(284) Angelica**

AUGUST

The grass and trees of the inland valleys lie still in the midday August heat. Most of the small streams and creeks have turned dry; what water there is has gone underground. The redwood forests leading to the coast collect moisture from the high fog that drifts inland, leaving wet imprints on the roads. To escape the heat one must turn west toward the ocean and explore the cool coastal canyons and headlands. The late summer flowers that started blooming near the end of July, the fragrant Mints and Tarweeds mixed with the white Yampah, show well against the burnt-gold countryside. By the middle of August, a subtle change in the early-morning light is occurring, reflecting fall-like colors from the grass and oaks: a tinge of red, a bit of yellow. Our unique Buckeye trees have already made the change from summer to fall with a display of reddish-brown leaves that will drop, leaving only the fruit by late September.

## (285) Scarlet Monkey Flower *(Mimulus cardinalis)*, 2 × A / S

**When:** *M. cardinalis* starts blooming in early July; by August, these lovely flowers of summer are in full color. The cycle of bloom for Scarlet Monkey Flowers lasts into early October (July – Oct.).

**Where:** Scarlet Monkey Flowers are found throughout the county, from the coast to the inner coastal mountain range, in wet moist canyons and hillside seeps. To find them, I look for water, if not on the surface at least in the ground, in seeps and drying riverbeds that are in full sun or partial shade. My favorite spot for locating these flowers is next to an old cistern fed by a hillside spring several miles from Ukiah on Orr Springs Road.

**What:** Scarlet Monkey Flower is a member of the Figwort family. I'm always amazed to see the brilliant red blooms of *M. cardinalis* braving the intense heat of summer in the burnt grass hills.

## (286) Humboldt County Fuchsia *(Epilobium septentrionale)*, A / S +

**When:** Humboldt County Fuchsia blooms near the middle of August; the cycle of bloom may last into early November (Aug. – Nov.).

**Where:** This species of Epilobium with the common name Fuchsia grows on rocky cliffs and outcrops from the coast to the inner coastal mountain range. I look for *E. septentrionale* in areas such as Robinson Creek Canyon west of Ukiah, and along Highway 101 on rocky outcroppings north of Laytonville. Another location is along the Eel River canyon near Dos Rios.

**What:** Humboldt County Fuchsia is a member of the Evening Primrose family. Another common name for it that I really like is "Hummingbird's Trumpet." The hummingbird, with its long slender beak, is able to extract nectar from the flower's long tubular base. Years ago, while hiking above 9,000 feet on Mt. Dana in Yosemite, I was captivated by the sight of hummingbirds feeding on a similar species called California Fuchsia *(Zauschneria californica)*. Astonishingly, the tiny birds seemed to have no trouble negotiating the thin air at that altitude.

## (287) Common Madia *(Madia elegans ssp. densifolia)*, A / S

**When:** *M. elegans* blooms by the middle of August, and in different regions of the county lasts well into October (Aug. – Oct.).

**Where:** From the coast to the inner mountains, Common Madia grows on dry grassy banks and hillsides. It's commonly seen along Highway 101 between Ukiah and Hopland, and along Route 175 several miles east of old Hopland. It also flourishes in Redwood Valley and Round Valley.

**What:** *M. elegans* is a lovely member of the Aster family. The flowers, with many yellow ray petals and dark reddish-brown centers, grow on branched stems reaching a height of three feet or more.

## (288) Shrubby Penstemon – Keckiella *(Keckiella corymbosa)*, A / S

**When:** You'll see Shrubby Penstemon blooming in late July; by August the scarlet petals will be in full color (July – Sept.).

**Where:** I'm always surprised and delighted to find Keckiella in full bloom during the dry month of August, but it's well suited to dry cliffs and rocky outcroppings from the coast to the inner coastal range. I find Shrubby Penstemon on the rocky walls along Mountain View Road, Fish Rock Road , and Pine Ridge Road. *K. corymbosa* also puts on a colorful show on Route 162 along the Eel River canyon.

**What:** A member of the Figwort family, Shrubby Penstemon is a small shrub-like plant with numerous small, red, fuchsia-shaped flowers blooming at the ends of thin woody stems.

# AUGUST

**(285) Scarlet Monkey Flower**

**(286) Humboldt County Fuchsia**

**(287) Common Madia**

**(288) Shrubby Penstemon**

## (289) Mountain Dogwood Berry *(Cornus nuttallii)*, 2 × A/S

**When:** It might be a little early to find the first Mountain Dogwood Berries in late August, but you'll surely notice the lovely fruit by mid-September (Aug.–Oct.).

**Where:** *C. nuttallii* inhabits the shady moist woodlands of mixed evergreen forests. Likely places to look for Mountain Dogwood Berries are Orr Springs Road, Highway 101 north of Willits, and the upper regions of Route 162 toward Mendocino Pass.

**What:** A member of the Dogwood family, *C. nuttallii* was described earlier (see photograph #71, page 49). We have several species of Dogwood in Mendocino County.

## (290) Fairy Bell Berries *(Disporum smithii)*, A/S

**When:** The beautiful orange berries of this small shrub-like plant enhance our woodlands by early August, and continue to do so well into September (Aug.–Sept.).

**Where:** Look for the berries of *D. smithii* in the shady woodlands on or near the coast. One of our favorite places is along the road into the Caspar Cemetery, off old Highway 1 just south of Caspar.

**What:** A small plant of the coastal forests, *D. smithii* is a member of the Lily family. The lovely fruit of Fairy Bells is every bit as attractive as its bell-shaped flowers (see photograph #92, page 59).

## (291) Clintonia Berries *(Clintonia andrewsiana)*, A/S

**When:** Clintonia berries form by early August and last into September (Aug.–Sept.).

**Where:** You'll find Clintonia Berries in the coastal redwoods, along the banks of many of our back roads as they near the coast. Orr Springs Road and the Branscomb Road to the coast have lovely displays of Clintonia berries.

**What:** The striking cobalt blue of Clintonia Berries is one of Nature's finest works. The beautiful blue berries are formed from the equally lovely red flowers of this enchanting member of the Lily family. (See photograph #153, page 93.)

## (292) Star Solomon Seal Berries *(Smilacina stellata)*, A/S

**When:** Look for the orange-red berries of Star Solomon Seal in early August, with some plants carrying berries into late September (Aug.–Sept.).

**Where:** *S. stellata* is found in the mixed coastal forests to the inner valley woodlands. Star Solomon Seal was described earlier (see photograph #81, page 54). You'll find the berries of many plants as attractive as the flowers that preceded them. It might be more difficult to spot the berries of *S. stellata* in the late summer and early fall than the flowers you saw blooming in April. The rich orange-red color of the berries may be hidden, as they tend to droop beneath the leaves.

**What:** *S. stellata* is a member of the Lily family.

**(289) Mountain Dogwood Berry**

**(290) Fairy Bell Berries**

**(291) Clintonia Berries**

**(292) Star Solomon Seal Berries**

## (293) Coastal Woolly Sunflower *(Eriophyllum lanatum var. arachnoideum)*, A/S

**When:** Eriophyllum blooms from July through September.

**Where:** *E. lanatum* is commonly found on the coastal headlands and in woodlands near the coast. Eriophyllum grows in Manchester Beach State Park and on the open bluffs north of Fort Bragg and MacKerricher State Park. I enjoy finding it blooming in late summer on the windswept bluffs above Alder Creek, at the north end of Manchester Beach State Park. The rich yellow petals are a welcome sight in late summer and early fall.

**What:** A member of the Aster family, the *E. lanatum* on the immediate coast is a low-growing prostrate plant. The long trailing stems rising at the tips produce lovely bouquets of small yellow flowers.

## (294) Honeysuckle Berries *(Lonicera hispidula)*, A/S

**When:** The fruit of the Honeysuckle first appears in August, and will remain on display in different parts of the county into late October.

**Where:** Honeysuckle Berries may be admired almost anywhere in the county, particularly along our wooded back roads and in the woodland foothills of the interior valleys.

**What:** The berries of this member of the Honeysuckle family are the fruit of the flowers that bloomed back in June (see photograph #208, page 121). On occasion, my wife and I see long strings of honeysuckle berries that resemble holiday ornaments hanging from roadside shrubs and trees.

## (295) Solomon Seal Berries *(Smilacina racemosa)*, A/S

**When:** The berries of Solomon Seal become noticeable by early August (Aug.–Sept.).

**Where:** *S. racemosa* is widespread throughout the county (see photograph #22, page 23). My wife and I enjoy looking for Solomon Seal berries while driving toward the coast, on such roads as Orr Springs Road and the Laytonville–Branscomb Road.

**What:** *S. racemosa* is a member of the Lily family.

## (296) Rattlesnake Orchid *(Goodyera oblongifolia)*, A/S

**When:** You'll find the Rattlesnake Orchid in bloom by mid-August or early September (Aug.–Sept.).

**Where:** *G. oblongifolia* grows in open forests west of Highway 101. I suggest searching toward the coast on Caspar–Little Lake Road, and in the State Forest Preserve, farther east on that same road.

**What:** *G. oblongifolia* is a member of the Orchid family. The common name, rattlesnake, seems to be derived from the mottling of the leaves, which resembles the markings on the skin of a rattler. The leaves are formed at the base of a six-to-twelve-inch spike-shaped stem supporting numerous small greenish-white blossoms. The flowers are difficult to see in the forest duff, so look for the exotically marked leaves.

**(293) Coastal Woolly Sunflower**

**(294) Honeysuckle Berries**

**(295) Solomon Seal  Berries**

**(296) Rattlesnake Orchid**

## (297) Aster *(Aster chilensis)*, A/S +

**When:** Look for this species of Aster to bloom in late August or September (Aug.–Oct.).

**Where:** A coastal plant, *A. chilensis* is found on ocean bluffs and along the road banks of Highway 1. Just south of Westport, a State Preserve has a turnout off Highway 1 that offers excellent parking. If you're on the North Coast, it's worth your while to stop and hike the trails down to the ocean. Along with a magnificent view of the coast, you'll find beautiful specimens of *A. chilensis*.

**What:** A member of the Aster family, *A. chilensis* grows to four feet tall in dense colonies. The colors of the ray-like flowers on its many ascending branches vary from purple to lavender, and sometimes white. The color display of *A. chilensis* is a late summer's gift.

## (298) Tansy Ragwort *(Senecio jacobaea)*, ½ A/S

**When:** Tansy Ragwort is noticeable in August and lasts well into November (Aug.–Nov.).

**Where:** Primarily a coastal plant, Tansy Ragwort has over the years made its way inland to the inner valleys and mountains.

**What:** A member of the Aster family, Senecio is a large, coarse weed that's poisonous to livestock. Its redeeming feature is the beautiful bouquets of yellow ray flowers that form large thickets of color. In the late fall Tansy Ragwort is quite noticeable in the inner valleys, as it's one of the last wildflowers still in bloom.

## (299) Golden Aster *(Heterotheca sessiliflora ssp. bolanderi)*, A/S

**When:** Golden Aster will make an appearance in late July or early August (Aug.–Oct.).

**Where:** Golden Aster is found immediately along the coast on ocean bluffs and headlands, and on stable dunes from Gualala north to Westport. It is common to areas such as the dunes of Ten Mile, at the northern end of the Haul Road. The photograph of Golden Aster on the opposite page was taken on those dunes, on a cold and rainy windswept October day.

**What:** A member of the Aster family, *H. sessiliflora* will colonize into large groups. The yellow flowers grow on recumbent stems (they trail along the ground and rise toward their tips). The numerous leaves and flowers crowded on the hairy stems give this plant a well-earned place on the unsheltered coast.

## (300) Hayfield Tarweed *(Hemizonia congesta)*, 1½ × A/S

**When:** Hayfield Tarweed usually appears around the third week in July, and reaches peak bloom by mid-August (Aug. –Sept.).

**Where:** *H. congesta* prefers the hot inland valley hillsides. I usually look for Hayfield Tarweed along the Boonville side of the Ukiah–Boonville Road, and along the grassy road banks of Highway 128 south of Boonville.

**What:** *H. congesta* is a member of the Aster family. You'll recognize something special when you savor the spicy fragrance of this late-blooming Tarweed.

# AUGUST

**(297) Aster**

**(298) Tansy Ragwort**

**(299) Golden Aster**

**(300) Hayfield Tarweed**

SEPTEMBER

The first rays of light from the rising sun break the stillness of early morning, casting golden firelight against the landscape. The daytime heat of summer is still with us, but the nights are cool now. The pear harvest is finishing and the grape harvest starting. September in Mendocino County will bring on a color change in our forests and grasslands, reminding us that we have entered our fall season. The leaves of the Poison Oak shrubs and vines have turned beautiful shades of red; they show us where not to go, but we can look. Acres of vineyards will start their dramatic change of color, from the deep green we have enjoyed all summer to the yellows, oranges, and reds of the wines they produce. The high inner mountains prepare for fall and winter; such a short summer for them. On the coast we have a mixture of fog and sun, and always the healing coolness. We no longer experience the great flower bloom of early spring and summer, but we can look forward with pleasure to the remaining flowers and berries still to come.

## (301) Evening Primrose *(Oenothera biennis)*, A/S

**When:** You'll find two different species of Evening Primrose still blooming in October (Aug.–Oct.).

**Where:** The two species of *Oenothera* that bloom in the county are found from the coast inland to the inner mountain range.

**What:** Native to eastern North America, *O. biennis* is common in Mendocino County and may easily be found along coastal strands and roadsides. *Oenothera wolfii*, similar in appearance, is rare in the county, but may also be found on the coast and inland to the inner mountains. Both species are members of the Evening Primrose family.

## (302) Vinegar Weed *(Trichostema lanceolatum)*, A/S

**When:** Vinegar weed blooms during the latter part of August, and continues blooming well into October (Aug.–Oct.).

**Where:** Often found but not really common in the county, Vinegar Weed inhabits the inner foothills, dry meadows and fields, and lives along some back roads. I look for it on the road into the Hopland Field Station.

**What:** *T. lanceolatum* is a member of the Mint family. The distinctive color and the pungent vinegar odor will draw your attention to this late-summer and early-fall bloomer. If you examine the many small flowers closely, you'll notice that the corolla tube is twisted and the stamens are curved back toward the stem. Vinegar Weed has a most interesting flower design, and numerous bees are attracted to its nectar.

## (303) Lessingia *(Lessingia nemaclada)*, A/S +

**When:** Lessingia usually blooms in late August or early September (Aug.–Oct.).

**Where:** Lessingia grows in the foothills and pine forests of the inner valleys. Although not prevalent in our county, it is scattered over a wide range. I find Lessingia growing on rocky open slopes in Low Gap County Park, and along the sides of Route 162 before Dos Rios.

**What:** Lessingia is a member of the Aster family. In Mendocino County, Lessingia is a dwarf—no more than eight inches tall—with small pink flower heads growing from twig-like stems. Lessingia assumes greater stature in the central and southern Sierra Nevada. My first encounter with it was in Yosemite Valley in late September during the early 1960s. In several open meadows, the numerous flowers created a sea of pale purple and lavender, a remarkable color display for that time of year.

## (304) Hawkbit *(Leontodon taraxacoides)*, A/S

**When:** Hawkbit blooms from late June into November.

**Where:** The yellow flowers of Hawkbit are found mostly on coastal headlands and bluffs.

**What:** Hawkbit is a member of the Aster family, as is the dandelion it resembles. *L. taraxacoides* migrated from Europe as a weed and is considered "alien." I've included it because it blooms late into October, adding a final touch to the fading colors of the coastal surroundings.

**(301) Evening Primrose**

**(302) Vinegar Weed**

**(303) Lessingia**

**(304) Hawkbit**

OCTOBER

Of all the months, October and November are perhaps the most beautiful. Having lived in Mendocino County for more than forty-five years I have learned to see the more subtle colors that blend on our hills and forests with a clarity that comes from spending many years in one place and being receptive to the natural beauty surrounding us. In October, the coastal grasses on the headlands of our rugged coast frame the browns and golds of our Gumplants and Buckwheat, which grow profusely to the very edge of the ocean. Canyon streams and rivers, ever running to the sea, are rich with the color yellow from the Maples and Willows that follow along their banks. The red berries and leaves of native Dogwood are highlighted in the darkness of our redwood forests, and on the tree-covered foothills and mountains, the Oaks turn the woodlands deep shades of orange and magenta. The sense of fall color in Mendocino is not overwhelming, but one of gentle browns and golds, with splashes of vibrant reds and yellows that lead the eye and capture the soul. As we turn toward the last few months of our journey, we find that October is the beginning of a beautiful light display, shown from early morning to late evening and lasting into winter.

## (305) Rose Hips *(Rosa sp.)*, A / S

**When:** By September the flowers of *Rosa sp.* will have formed into the fruit commonly called Rose Hips (Sept.– Nov.).

**Where:** I believe the photograph on the opposite page is *Rosa eglanteria*, or Sweet Brier Eglantine, a garden escapee. You'll find marvelous large shrubs of Rose Hips in the open fields and along the fence lines of the Sherwood Road west of Willits. Many of our coastal headlands contain fine displays of Rose Hips, as do the woodlands and fields of the inner valleys and mountains.

**What:** Rose Hips vary in size and shape depending on the species. I chose the photograph on the opposite page because it depicts the rich color and size of some of the many species of Rose Hips. Because of their high vitamin C content and excellent blending qualities, Rose Hips have been used for many years in the making of fine teas throughout the world.

## (306) Fringed Corn Lily *(Veratrum fimbriatum)*, ½ A / S

**When:** *V. fimbriatum* blooms in late September, the flowering cycle lasting into early November.

**Where:** Fringed Corn Lily is a coastal plant that grows near Highway 1, close to seeps and bogs and in the understory of mixed evergreen forests and high grass. My wife and I find *V. fimbriatum* alongside Highway 1 several miles north of Anchor Bay, along the Old Stage Road on the eastern ridge above Gualala, and in Russian Gulch State Park.

**What:** A member of the Lily family, *V. fimbriatum* has stamens marked in deep yellow, with the outer edge of the petals cut into intricate fringes, as though snipped by some forest creature. The plant may reach a height of three feet on a corn-like stalk; the slender leaves are already brown by the time the flowers bloom. For months on end the interesting leaves, green and deeply veined, are visible, but nothing seems to happen, making you wonder what plant this is. Don't give up — the unique blossoms will reward you in early October, and all is forgiven.

## (307) California Wild Grape *(Vitis californica)*, ¾ A / S

**When:** During the months of September through November, wild grape leaves turn lovely shades of red and gold that equal our finest autumn colors (Sept.– Nov.).

**Where:** Wild Grape is found throughout the county. In the late fall we particularly enjoy driving on woodland back roads that follow creeks and streams where the intense hues of wild grape light up the darkened roadsides. During the fall months, roads like Orr Springs and Laytonville to Branscomb are rich with the colors of wild grape.

**What:** Native to California, *V. californica* is a member of the Grape family. Because of the climbing ability of the vines, the large leaves are found high in the trees and brush, resulting in stunning colors above eye level.

## (308) Scarlet Monkey Flower *(Mimulus cardinalis)*, 1½ × A / S

**When:** Scarlet Monkey Flower blooms from July through October.

**Where:** See photograph #285, page 165.

**What:** *M. cardinalis* is a member of the Figwort family. I've included it again because, while hiking on Low Gap Road early one morning in October 1992, I turned up a rather steep dry creek bed and spotted a dab of brilliant red illuminated by the early light. I managed to get my camera gear and myself through a narrow opening in the rock-strewn creek. A trickle of water led to a small seep and a bouquet of Monkey Flowers. The light lasted less than a minute, but allowed the image on the opposite page.

**(305) Rose Hips**

**(306) Fringed Corn Lily**

**(307) California Wild Grape**

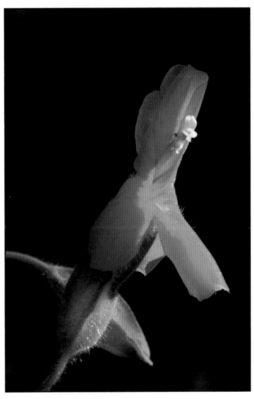

**(308) Scarlet Monkey Flower**

# NOVEMBER

By November, the first light rains have washed the dust from our back roads, and the county is becoming festive in preparation for the coming holidays. The glorious colors of fall are reaching their peak in the vineyards; many leaves are already on the ground, revealing the twisted black vines beneath. After a rain the foothills are damp, and the smell of the earth mingles with the pungent odor of the Oaks and Pepperwoods. Hiking the side hill forests is a color treat, as the red-orange hue of the Oak and Madrone leaves scatters in the wind, back-lit by the soft November light. The coastal headlands and prairies have returned to a winter sleep, ending the great flower display for another year. The colors are best seen on many of our back roads, where the cool green forests and canyon streams are ignited with splashes of yellow from the Maples and Willows. The inland valleys' fields and meadows, ringed by great Oaks, offer stunning displays in November's gentle light. We have received a wonderful gift from Nature: a color tapestry imprinted forever in our hearts and minds, so that although far away, we may once again visit this magical place called Mendocino.

## (309) Coyote Bush *(Baccharis pilularis)*, A / S

**When:** Coyote Bush blooms in late October and reaches the peak of its flowering cycle by mid-December (Sept.–Dec.).

**Where:** Coyote Bush is found throughout Mendocino County, from the coastal headlands to the wooded and open foothills of the inner valleys.

**What:** A member of the Aster family, *B. pilularis* is a shrub that may reach a height of more than eight feet. By October, the light-green foliage is covered with small, silky, white flower clusters that remain for several months, eventually opening and scattering seedpods resembling fine-spun hair. At Christmastime many years ago, I decorated our house with some cuttings of Coyote Bush and Toyon Berries. Having had no experience with *B. pilularis*, but liking the grayish white of its silky flowers, I assembled pinecones and Toyon berries and topped them off with a sprig from my unknown shrub. I made five of these ornaments and placed them around the living room. Early one morning several days later, I walked into the room to congratulate myself on my beautiful decorations and, to my horror, found the room filled with small floating seed vessels—my shrub had decided it was time to propagate. I was never able to get all of the silky flower seeds out of the furnishings, and when anyone walked into the room it would start a miniature snowstorm that would stick to clothing, hair, and anything else that might be available—including the dog and cat.

## (310) Madrone Berries *(Arbutus menziesii)*, ½ A / S

**When:** Madrone Berries appear during early November and reach their peak display by mid-December (Nov.–Dec.).

**Where:** Widespread throughout our county, the Madrone tree is found in the foothills and woodlands.

**What:** The Madrone is a member of the Heath family. Its beautiful display of salmon-to-red-colored berries in late fall and early winter is not to be forgotten (see photograph #83, page 55).

## (311) Toyon Berries – Christmas Berries *(Heteromeles arbutifolia)*, A / S

**When:** The beautiful red-to-scarlet Toyon Berries are evident from October into the New Year.

**Where:** Toyon shrubs are found in all parts of our county.

**What:** *H. arbutifolia* is a member of the Rose family.

## (312) Buckeye Fruit *(Aesculus californica)*, A / S

**When:** You'll notice the fruit of the Buckeye on the ground by late October and early November (Nov.–Dec.).

**Where:** *A. californica* is found throughout Mendocino County.

**What:** I'll always enjoy looking for the polished fruit of the Buckeye tree during the month of November. I watch for the long root that eventually cracks open the Buckeye ball and then finds its way into the ground—a sometimes perilous journey, depending on where and how the fruit lands (see photograph #159, page 95).

**(309) Coyote Bush**

**(310) Madrone Berries**

**(311) Toyon Berries**

**(312) Buckeye Fruit**

# DECEMBER

The month of December has arrived. The small cities and towns are brightly lit with hometown lights and decorations in celebration of Christmas and the coming New Year. In the wooded foothills and forests, the Madrone trees and Toyon shrubs put on their own magnificent show with great masses of red berries. The Buckeye trees — early to green and first to brown — have produced a golden chestnut-like treasure, polished and shining, a lovely ornament for Nature's winter garden. While on a country road in the gloom of early evening, a sudden glint will catch your eye; as you look more closely in the gathering dusk, the pure white of the Snowberry sends forth its winter charm. We have arrived at the end of our adventure and have forgotten many of the wonderful things we have seen, but it really doesn't matter, because we have shared in Nature's timeless voyage of rebirth and renewal. We have received a gift of love: the understanding that Nature's journey never ends, that we are all joined together in the amazing adventure called life.

**When:** Snowberries first appear in late October and stay with us through February. I've chosen to put them in the month of December because they fit the winter landscape (Oct.–Feb.).

**Where:** The Snowberry grows in nearly all regions of the county. My wife and I look for these plants along many of the county back roads, in open brush following old fence lines, or in shaded woods near creeks and streams. Highway 128 west of Boonville, the Sherwood Road north of Willits, and Orr Springs Road, offer fine displays of Snowberries.

**What:** *S. albus*, or common Snowberry, is a member of the Honeysuckle family. The shrub-like plant with open branched stems may reach a height of four to five feet. The flowers are pinkish-white, tiny, and difficult to see. The white berries that appear in early October and last well into late February brighten many of our back roads during the early winter months. Sadly, the fruit of the Snowberry is toxic to humans.

Most of Mendocino County was in the midst of a cold snap early in December 1994. Wanting a rural winter setting with Snowberries as the theme, I left Ukiah before sunrise and drove to the Sherwood Road northwest of Willits, hoping to find some Snowberries covered with ice. I arrived at my destination later than I'd planned; the sun was already up and melting the ice that had formed overnight. I located a thicket where several Snowberry plants were growing, found what I felt might work as a photograph—a combination of leaf, berries, and melting ice—and took the image on the opposite page.

# DECEMBER

**(313) Snowberry**

# GLOSSARY

**California Coastal Range:** Includes the mountains ranging from the coast to those on the eastern boundary of the county.

### Subcategories

*Inner Mountains:* The Inner California Coastal Range refers to the mountains located between Highway 101 and the eastern boundary of the county. Mendocino National Forest is located in the inner mountain range.

*High Country Inner Mountains:* Mountains from five to 7,000 feet in elevation, located in the northeast section of the county; called "High Mountains of the Inner Coastal Range."

*Outer Mountains:* Refers to the smaller mountains, located on the western side of Mendocino County, which separate the coast from the inner valleys, mostly located west of Highway 101.

**Bract:** A modified leaf, in some cases brightly colored, growing at the base or on the stalk of a flower.

**Canyon Streams:** Streams that find their way to the ocean through cuts in the forests and hills, usually in steep country.

**Chaparral:** A thicket of shrubs and thorny bushes.

**Coastal Headlands:** The open meadows directly above the coastal cliffs.

**Coastal Prairies:** Large open grasslands just east of the coastal headlands.

**Creek (seasonal):** A small stream that will usually go dry or underground during the summer months.

**Cycle of Bloom:** A period of time when flowers of the same species complete their bloom in different areas of the county.

**Foothill Woodlands:** The hills of the inner valleys that have open canopies of Oak, Madrone, Manzanita, etc., and a herbaceous grassy understory.

**Habitat:** The region where a plant or animal naturally grows or lives, native environment.

**Herb:** Any seed plant whose stem withers to the ground after each season's growth.

**High Grass Hills:** Open hill country, usually in the interior valleys, where the grass exceeds two feet in height.

**Inner Valleys:** Includes all valleys of open land inland from the coast; for example, Boonville, Ukiah, Potter Valley, Willits, and Round Valley.

**Outcroppings, Rocky:** Appear at the surface, as a rock formation appears unexpectedly at the earth's surface.

**Seeps:** Wet areas, usually from springs that ooze water through the spring and summer months.

**Side Hills:** Steep hillsides, either open grass or wooded.

**Strand:** Open land on a level with the coastal shoreline where the water has receded.

**Streams:** Small, moving bodies of water that run into the larger rivers.

**Umbel:** A cluster of flowers with stalks of the same length that spring from the same point.

# ACKNOWLEDGMENTS

I would like to thank my wife, Robbie Stearns, for being my friend and companion throughout our adventure in *A Journey In Time*. You were with me every step of the way, Robbie.

Without Kerry Heise, Botanist, U.C. Hopland Research and Extension Center, *A Journey In Time* could not have been written. He was steadfast as both botanist and friend, and I look forward to many more years of friendship with Kerry, his wife, Adina, and their lovely children.

I chose Cypress House of Fort Bragg to guide me through the morass of publishing *A Journey In Time*, and so they did. Owner Cynthia Frank led the way with her intelligence and compassion, and designer Michael Brechner expressed himself through his digital genius. To the entire gang at Cypress House, thank you.

Joe Shaw was superlative in making me sound as though I could write. During our association as author and editor, Robbie and I have become best friends with Joe. I will always be grateful for his clear thinking, caring suggestions, and continuing friendship.

Geologist Julie Bawcom condensed the geology of Mendocino County into several paragraphs, no easy task, so we could have a geology section for simple edification. CDF personnel in Anderson Valley were alerted to keep an eye out for the rare plants, which they did generously.

Rixanne Wehren, premiere mapmaker, owner of GeoGraphics on Albion Ridge Road, and designer of the beautiful map for *A Journey In Time*, thank you.

Without the kindness of the U. S. Forest Service staff in Round Valley, Covelo, California, *A Journey In Time* would be half a book. Their interest and friendship guided me through four years of exploring and photographing the high-mountain wildflowers of the inner coastal range. Thank you, guys and gals.

The Lab in Santa Rosa, The Lightroom in Berkeley, and Triple S Camera in Ukiah all contributed greatly to the professional work evident in the photographs presented in these pages. Their technical advice and friendship guided me through examining a decade of slides for quality and excellence.

More of the many people who helped me create a book about Mendocino County's wildflowers and its incomparable beauty: Dr. Robert Werra, for helping me locate flowers; Ansley Coale and Larry Thomas, for allowing me to photograph on their property; Valerie Brownrigg, who made me computer literate and designed my Web site; Evan Johnson, Bill Johnson, and Tom Liden, for their encouragement; Beth Campbell, owner of Moonlight Framer, who has shown my work in her gallery for years, the unnamed employees of our State Parks, who were helpful in so many ways, and to all the other wonderful people my wife and I have met on our journey, thank you.

# BIBLIOGRAPHY

**Alt**, David D., and Donald W. Hyndman. *Roadside Geology*. Missoula, Montana: Mountain Press Publishing Co., 1975.

**Balls**, Edward K. *Early Uses of California Plants*. Berkeley & Los Angeles, Ca: University of California Press, 1962.

**Crampton**, Beecher. *Grasses in California*. Berkeley & Los Angeles, Ca: University of California Press, 1974.

**Dobelis**, Inge N., ed. *Magic and Medicine of Plants*. Pleasantville, NY: The Reader's Digest Association, Inc., 1986.

**Hickman**, James C., ed. *The Jepson Manual, Higher Plants of California*. Berkeley, Ca: University of California Press, 1993.

**Horn**, Elizabeth L. *Wildflowers 3*. Beaverton, Oregon: The Touchstone Press, 1976.

**Munz**, Philip A. *California Mountain Wildflowers*. Berkeley & Los Angeles, Ca: University of California Press, 1963.

**Munz**, Philip A. *California Spring Wildflowers*. Berkeley & Los Angeles, Ca: University of California Press, 1961.

**Munz**, Philip A. *Shore Wildflowers*. Berkeley & Los Angeles, Ca: University of California Press, 1964.

**Niehaus**, Theodore F., and Charles L. Ripper. *A Field Guide to Pacific States Wildflowers*. Boston, Mass: Houghton Mifflin Company, 1976.

**Parsons**, Mary Elizabeth. *The Wildflowers of California*. San Francisco, Ca: H. S. Crocker Company, 1918.

**Smith**, Gladys L., and Clare R. Wheeler. *A Flora of the Vascular Plants of Mendocino County, California*. San Francisco, Ca: The University of San Francisco, 1990.

**Spellenberg**, Richard. *The Audubon Society Field Guide to North American Wildflowers*. New York: Alfred A. Knopf, Inc., 1979.

**Stewart**, Charles. *Wildflowers of the Olympics and Cascades*. Port Angeles, Wash: Nature Education Enterprises, 1988.

**Strickler**, Dr. Dee. *Alpine Wildflowers*. Columbia Falls, Montana: The Flower Press, 1990.

**Venning**, Frank D. *A Guide to Field Identification, Wildflowers of North America*. New York: Golden Press, 1984.

**Walton**, David. *The FOCALGUIDE to Plants and Flowers*. New York & London: Focal Press Limited, 1979.

**Young**, Dorothy King. *Redwood Empire Wildflower Jewels*. Healdsburg, Ca: Naturegraph Publishers, 1970.

# ABOUT THE PHOTOS

## Equipment

### Land- and Seascapes

Pentax 67 camera, 45, 90, 200mm lenses, Benbo tripod, 120 film, Velvia slide film. Nikon FM2 camera, 35–200mm zoom lens, 35mm Velvia slide film.

### Flower Photos

Nikon FM2 camera, 105mm macro lens, Benbo tripod, 35mm film, Velvia slide film.

## Photographs

*Page viii* • **Bend in the Road** — A special bend on Low Gap Road produced one of my favorite images, this photo of the road taken in the early-morning light of September 1993.

*Page x* • **Barn on Fish Rock Road** — This image of the barn was taken in early February 1995, looking through dormant trees.

*Page xi* • **Anderson Valley** — September afternoon light flashed across the valley, producing a lovely panorama of grasslands, trees, and hills.

*Page 2* • **Mist in the Mountains** — Early-morning light, and mist lying between two mountain ridges off Low Gap Road, allowed me to shoot the dramatic fall colors of October 1998.

*Page 6* • **Old Ranch Barn** — Storm conditions and beautiful light produced this image of a Mendocino County barn built in the early 1900s.

*Page 7* • **Toward Westport** — A foggy, windswept day produced this image. I shot it on the headlands above Chadburn Gulch, several miles south of Westport.

*Page 10* • **Gold Vineyard** — Soft, direct February light ignited the vineyard when I took this shot, my camera facing east toward the Russian River and the Mayacmas Mountains.

*Page 11* • **Manzanita in the Rain** — I shot this image of a beautiful Manzanita in mist-like rain off Low Gap Road. The rain saturated the trunk into glistening shades of polished mahogany.

*Page 18* • **Mendocino Village** — A March storm along the coast produced dark clouds and shafts of light over Mendocino. I snapped the photo from the headlands southwest of the village.

*Page 19* • **Green Hills and Barn** — Several miles south of Ukiah, I positioned my camera and tripod looking east at the barn and green hills; Highway 101 is hidden behind the foreground hill.

*Page 40* • **Trail in Van Damme** — In early April I hiked several miles on the Fern Canyon Trail in Van Damme State Park. I turned westward and, with the coastal forest backlit, took the shot.

*Page 41* • **Flowers on Mountain House** — Wildflowers covered a side hill in a blaze of yellow on Mountain House Road in late April 1998.

*Page 72* • **Rancheria Wildflowers** — The little meadow next to Orr Springs Road was filled with the color of Owl's Clover, Poppies, and Lupine when I took the shot in May 1999.

*Page 73* • **Jefferson Way Headlands** — One of my favorite spots on the coast, Jefferson Way headlands is located off Jefferson Way Road south of Fort Bragg. The photo was taken looking north.

*Page 112* • **Redwoods in the Mist** — I was hiking in Montgomery Woods State Reserve on a June morning; when a low-hanging fog lifted slightly, I took the photo looking north up the east side trail.

*Page 113* • **Coastal Bluffs** — Taken south of Schooner Gulch in late June 2002—a bit of fog, ocean, and bluff in full glorious bloom; the camera and tripod were facing north.

*Page 134* • **Anthony Peak** — This image was taken in late July 2001, with the camera and tripod facing north toward the Yolla Bolly Wilderness.

*Page 135* • **July Hills** — This photo reflects the burnt gold color of grass in July. The image was taken looking west on Low Gap Road in mid-morning.

*Page 162* • **August Hills** — The "dog days" of summer mean August in Mendocino County. I shot this image from Road 253 (Boonville–Ukiah), looking east in the late afternoon.

Page 163 • **The Path** — I walk in Low Gap County Park throughout the year. "The Path" was taken on the southeast trail, the morning light reflecting the color of early fall in the grass and trees.

Page 172 • **Grass on Big River** — The yellow-orange clumps of grass along the Big River headwaters have always fascinated me. I took the photo in September 2000.

Page 173 • **Oak Grove, Early-morning Light** — While walking on Low Gap Road over a period of years, I always passed this grove of oak trees. The photo was taken with the rising sun in 1996.

Page 176 • **Eel River in the Fall** — The cottonwoods and willows and their reflection in the river, taken south of Dos Rios in October 2000.

Page 177 • **Yellow Leaves and Black Oaks** — The photo of the stunning yellow and orange leaves of oak trees, backlit by morning light, was taken on Low Gap Road in October 1994.

Page 180 • **November Vineyard** — Taken south of Ukiah during a storm in 1994. I pointed my camera east, a shaft of light ignited the cottonwoods, I had my photo.

Page 181 • **Orr Springs Road** — The image was taken in November 1994, several miles west of Orr Springs Resort in an area I call "seep spring."

Page 184 • **December Vineyard** — The image of snow-covered vineyard and hills was taken in December 2001 in the same location as "November Vineyard."

Page 185 • **Woodland Mist** — The photo of leafless trees and mossy oaks was taken on Low Gap Road in December 1994; the winter grass was already turning green.

Page 192 • **Poison Oak Leaves in the Forest** — Early-morning light filtered down through the Montgomery Woods State Reserve redwoods when I snapped this beautiful but dangerous image.

# INDEX

194